A CLASSIC EXCELLENCE

A Framework of Education Based on Christ,
Derived From the Bible.

A Classic Excellence

Copyright © 2005 by F. Chapin Marsh III EdD
Published by Calvary Chapel Publishing (CCP),
a resource ministry of Calvary Chapel of Costa Mesa
3800 South Fairview Rd.
Santa Ana, CA 92704

All rights reserved. No part of this publication may be reproduced, stored in a retrieval system, or transmitted in any form by any means, electronic, mechanical, photocopy, recording, or otherwise, without the prior permission of the publisher, except as provided by USA copyright law.

First printing, 2005

All Scripture quotations in this book, unless otherwise indicated, are taken from the *New King James Version*. Copyright © 1982, Thomas Nelson, Inc. Used by permission. All rights reserved.

ISBN 1-59751-018-1

Printed in the United States of America.

Table Of Contents

	Foreword	5
	Introduction	9
one	Basic Excellence	23
two	Just Jesus	37
three	Foundational Excellence	61
four	Leadership And Love	81
five	Functional Excellence	103
six	Fundamentals Of Excellence	115
seven	Standards Of Excellence	123
eight	Cornerstones Of Excellence	165
nine	Classroom Excellence	179
ten	Operational Excellence	205
eleven	Distinctive Excellence	227
twelve	Technological Excellence	241
thirteen	Traditions In Excellence	247
fourteen	Cost Of Excellence	265
fifteen	Eternal Excellence	275

Foreword

Christian education is at a crossroad. One of the paths trodden by some Christian educators is simply to copy the government schools and add a Bible class or a chapel to the public educational frameworks. This, of course, seldom works in that the worldview espoused by the frameworks does not align itself with the Bible. Additionally, the pedagogy of public frameworks, though helpful, is not always thorough and takes a distinctly progressive tone, especially in relation to History, Science, and English. Another path taken by some is to invent some new format or theory of education and pray that it works. Of course this road leads to hardship in that many of these new theories are untested, un-researched, and suspect in their scope and agenda; and ultimately it is the student who suffers as these uncharted waters are sailed.

So, what is the Christian, serious about their faith, to do? Well, the answer is simple: turn to the Bible. Two years ago I wrote a book entitled *The Master Teacher: Developing a Christ-Based Philosophy of Education.* In this book, I challenged the educator and pastor to look closely at the person of Jesus found in Scripture when constructing a philosophy of education. I encouraged the reader to seek a framework of education based upon Christ's commands and actions derived from the Bible, and not just reformulate a government (or any non-biblical) school-based model when implementing curriculum or starting a school. In this work, my intention was to highlight the fact that there are four distinct areas emphasized in the "schooling" of Jesus and in His teaching. These elements are the body, mind, soul, and social action. It is upon these four areas, I argue, that Christian schools should develop their educational environment and framework.

Since the writing of that book, several exciting elements have occurred within the Calvary Chapel movement, of which I and the author of this present volume, Dr. Chapin Marsh, are a part. First, an on-going dialogue has flowered between several Calvary Chapel schools. The conversations, ideas, and encouragement have been an exciting thing to behold. The Lord has richly blessed Calvary Chapels with wonderful servant-leaders. Second, an association, CCEA, has been initiated to help assist schools in developing Christian schools within the Calvary Chapel movement. Third, national and upcoming regional conferences are being held to aid schools in the education process. Fourth, literature (of which this is handbook is a part) and other resource helps (scope and sequence, tapes, etc.) are being made available to the schools in their educational ministry. However, the greatest element of the endeavor has been to see the Lord work in the lives of His people, utilizing them to impact the next generation.

This handbook you are about to read is the first installment of CCEA's endeavor to equip the Christian school movement within Calvary Chapels. Its focus is simple: To give biblical and practical advice on how to implement a Christ-based philosophy of education. My good friend, Dr. Chapin Marsh, is a master in helping schools to garner vision and set goals. He gives sound, biblical direction in developing a truly Christ-based educational framework. In this handbook you will find solid advice from one who has prayerfully, carefully, and biblically, set out to minister to educators. As you read through this work, ask yourself how you can implement the truths and practical aid found within its pages; and most importantly, ask the Lord to give you a passion for education and the shaping of the minds, bodies, and souls of the students you minister to, trusting the Lord to accomplish wonderful things in your Christian school!

In conclusion, as opposed to a government school or

an untested educational path, I present to you a third way: Christ-based education where the Bible leads and the truths that transform your educational ministries are found within its very pages.

May the Lord be glorified, and your ministries richly blessed!

Grace and peace,
Brian C. Nixon

Introduction

This is an invitation to an educational revolution. It is for board members, administrators, teachers, aides, parents, students, politicians, home-schoolers, and anyone desiring a distinctively Christian approach to excellence in Christian education. This is a message that Christian schools can be lighthouses of excellence rather than fading glimmers of hope in a sick and decaying world.

The secular world is dying. As public schools aggressively promote anti-biblical approaches to life and learning, Horace Mann, the father of modern public schools, would be proud. He envisioned educational institutions to be temples of new humanism. Here, man would be at the center, controlling his destiny apart from, and often in opposition to, God. Is it any wonder new Christian schools are opening doors at the rate of three a day worldwide?

A Classic Excellence is not another how-to manual. Instead, it addresses day-to-day operational issues facing Christian schools. Specific and difficult issues are addressed with candor. *A Classic Excellence* is intended to elicit dialogue within each Christian school community.

On his missionary journeys the apostle Paul not only planted churches, but he maintained the ministry of rebuking and exhorting those already in existence. *A Classic Excellence* seeks to promote the type of excitement and introspection that Paul was called to. It is written to encourage the enthusiasm accompanying spiritual insights from God. May the ideas you encounter here promote other new ideas as the Lord is given free reign to quicken hearts and minds in your particular school situation.

This is also a reminder that you are not alone. So much

of what you experience in Christian education may feel peculiar to you. Poor decision making, attacks from within, miscommunication, and much more affect everyone in the Christian school movement. Here, we shed light on these types of experiences, so often marked by trial and turmoil.

Here also is guided reflection. Interpersonal conflict in any organization can be difficult. In Christian organizations it can be exacerbated by the expectation of "We are Christians and should treat each other better than the world." Unfortunately, however, Christians can be some of the most vitriolic and mean-spirited people to deal with. Indeed, conflict in Christian schools often leaves folks scratching their heads in amazement. We would all do well to remember that we are sinners, teaching sinners, whose parents are sinners. Rest easy, my friend, you are not alone.

A Classic Excellence is also created as a living, breathing reference. Here are ideas to stimulate Christian educators towards an active, passionate excellence. God may use you, the reader, as a catalyst for change in your Christian school. In some cases the school administrator or a board member may introduce the concepts of this work into the Christian school culture. Christian education is on the verge of turning the corner from a stopgap alternative to a world class excellence. That type of excellence does not come without significant commitment.

The reader will be faced with making a definite choice. That choice entails answering two simple questions: First, "Is God speaking to you through the material in this book?" Second, "Will you have the courage and faith to step out and obey what God is telling you?" Actually, the choice is a little like life itself.

A Classic Excellence is defined as an uncompromising vision for fundamental and distinctive God-breathed excellence in all areas of Christian education. It includes students reading in kindergarten; second language and technology classes offered for kindergarten through the twelfth grades; school discipline that is biblical, corrective, and consistent; and reading, writing, history, and arithmetic taught from a Christian viewpoint with vigor and no apologies.

In short, it might sound something like this: "A 1950s style, Dwight D. Eisenhower, values-based, technology-driven, Christ-centered school." Christian schools promoting a classic excellence will be well positioned at the vanguard of the next move of God in the lives of youth worldwide. Christian education must break free of limited expectations and negative perceptions. Christian education is at a crossroads. Indeed, "our expectations are our only limitations."

What Is Christian Education?

Christian schools are the spiritual training centers for the next generation. Christian education is the most important and powerful tool at the church's disposal to evangelize and disciple young people today. Those called into the Christian school movement must begin a fearless and relentless pursuit of distinctives leading to a classic excellence in Christian education. God is using Christian schools to raise up a godly remnant in the last days. Christian students, more than ever, need a safe place in which to learn the full counsel of God.

Some Christian schools have emerged as a response to fear. Parents want to protect their children from violence, forced busing, anti-God philosophy, and other negative influences found in the public schools. The result, then, is a mindset within Christian schools that they are supposedly fulfilling their mandate as long as students are taught the

Bible, and children are protected from violence and anti-biblical philosophies. But this is no longer enough.

God is moving in Christian schools, and God deserves the very best. There is a God-breathed, orderly, and effective manner in which to open and operate a high quality Christian school. Christian schools should set out to meet that challenge. Times and technology are moving at a very rapid rate. This book is designed to be an encouragement and a resource to help you and your school.

Pray as you read. Be prepared for God to use something in this book to spark an original idea in your mind. Take the opportunity to bounce ideas off friends and colleagues. Identify and discuss the distinctives of excellence already established within your Christian school.

The vision both to begin and then to operate each Christian school is unique. The enemy, Satan, will stop at nothing to destroy ministry to God's children. It is a life and death proposition. Remember how Pharaoh tried to kill all the babies when Moses was born? Baby Moses, floating in a handmade basket, carried God's vision to deliver those in bondage and to set His people free. Moses represented God's plan for the next generation. Christian schools today reflect the same basket of protection for our next generation.

Consider also Herod, who killed children in anticipation of Jesus' birth and the realization of God's new covenant. Jesus, of course, represented grace triumphing over judgment. Jesus' parents sacrificed so much to bring Him, God's vision, to birth in that Bethlehem stable. Today Christian parents offer similar sacrifices to send their children to Christian schools. In both instances the enemy, Satan, killed many innocent children in an attempt to thwart God's vision for the following generation.

Attack will come against Christian schools. The oldest

device the Enemy uses is divide-and-conquer. He did it in the garden. Remember how the Serpent asked Eve, "Has God indeed said?"

Eve, being away from her husband, engaged the Serpent in dialogue. The end result was Eve's distraction from the multiple blessings God had given her and Adam. She began to focus on the one thing God said not to eat. In fact, she not only focused on it, she began to impute wrong motives upon God. Satan had tricked Eve into thinking God had selfish motives toward her and Adam. "For God knows that in the day you eat of it your eyes will be opened, and you will be like God, knowing good and evil" (Gen. 3:5). The irony is that the one thing God said not to do was not for His own benefit, but for Adam and Eve's protection.

Christians in Christian schools can be snared in a similar trap. It is important that those in Christian schools do not succumb to the attitude of us versus them, or pitting, unhealthily, one school against another. Each Christian school is unique and special to God. Christian schools working together, not apart, can do much good for the kingdom of God. Our witness to a dying world is at stake.

Celebrate God's call, don't compare ministries, be faithful in the little things, and rejoice always. God will fulfill the ministry He has called into being. "He who calls you is faithful, who also will do it" (1 Thess. 5:24). God will surprise you. Let Him.

A missionary to India told the following story at an annual ministry conference. It is particularly meaningful for Christian schools struggling to find their niche. It is always best to keep our focus vertical rather than horizontal. Remember to always "look up." Up is where God places the vision, protection, and provision for each of our schools.

A water bearer carried two large pots; one hung on each

end of a pole, which he laid across the water bearer's neck. One of the pots had a crack in it, and while the other pot was perfect and always delivered a full portion of water at the end of a long walk from the stream to the master's house, the cracked pot arrived only half full.

For a full two years this went on daily, with the bearer delivering only one and a half pots of water to his master's house. Of course the perfect pot was proud of its accomplishments. It was perfect to the end for which it was made. But the poor cracked pot was ashamed of its own imperfection, and miserable that it was able to accomplish only half of what it was made to do.

After two years of what it perceived to be bitter failure, the cracked pot spoke to the water bearer one day by the stream. "I am ashamed of myself, and I want to apologize to you." "Why?" asked the bearer. "What are you ashamed of?"

"I have been able, for these past two years, to deliver only half my load because this crack in my side causes water to leak out all the way back to your master's house. Because of my flaws, you have to do all of this work, and you don't get full value from your efforts," the pot said.

The water bearer felt sorry for the old cracked pot, and in his compassion he said, "As we return from the master's house, I want you to notice the beautiful flowers along the path."

Indeed, as they went up the hill, the old cracked pot took notice of the sun warming the beautiful wild flowers on the side of the path, and this cheered it some. But at the end of the trail, it still felt bad because it leaked out half its load, and so again the pot apologized to the bearer for its failure.

The bearer said to the pot, "Did you notice that there were flowers only on your side of the path, but not on the other pot's side? That's because I have always known about your flaw, and I took advantage of it. I planted flower seeds on your side of the path, and every day while we walk back from the stream, you've watered them. For two years I have been able to pick these beautiful flowers to decorate my master's table. Without you being just the way you are, he would not have this beauty to grace his house."

Imagine for a moment that God may be unlocking the purpose and provision for your Christian school. Expect to be blessed!

A Christian School History

Paul Kienel, in his book *A History of Christian School History*, writes, "Christian school education was prominent among the early church Christians in Rome and in other cities in the Roman Empire" (xiii). Also, Kienel was surprised to discover that

> *Christian school education was much larger in the past than I ever dreamed it was and that we have, as a movement of Christian educators, spiritual ancestors whose exploits and heroic deeds demand our utmost reverence and gratitude. I must confess that I wept numerous times as I read and wrote about the catacomb dwellers in Rome and their school for martyrs and those amazing Waldensian Christians who for centuries provided clandestine Christian schools for their children in the rocks and caves of the Italian Alps. I was deeply moved as I wrote about John Huss, president of Prague University, who defied medieval Catholic authorities by publishing the Bible in the language of his fellow Bohemians and was burned at the stake for doing so. Until my research uncovered it, I was unaware that*

16   A Classic Excellence

> *John Huss and his followers established hundreds of Christian schools in his homeland a hundred years before the Great Reformation in 1517. You would weep as I did when I saw Belgium's memorial to William Tyndale, who was choked and burned at the stake for translating the Bible into the English language.*
>
> *I learned that the great church reformers—Martin Luther, John Calvin, John Knox, Ulrich Zwingli, and others—gave as much energy to establishing Christian schools as they gave to reforming the church. To them Christian school education and church reform were inseparable allies. Neither, they believed, could succeed without the other.* (xiii–xiv)

A history of Christian education is really a cyclical yet familiar dilemma. Like modern day Christian parents, the early Christians "felt little need for the type of intellectual education provided by the Roman schools, and the character of the educated society about them, as they saw it, did not make them wish for the so-called pagan learning." (Cubberly 93 from Kienel 3)

Likewise, early church parents living in Rome shared a similar disdain for the public state schools that many Christian parents feel today:

> *They were bitterly opposed to the subjects taught in the pagan schools, and blamed pagan culture for the vices and corruption of pagan society. To them its literature was full of impurities; its art depicted immoralities and was associated with immoral religions; its philosophy undermined and destroyed Christian faith, because it led to trusting one's own wisdom … the pagan school was the enemy of the*

church, and its curriculum was to be despised by all true believers .... Physical training, literature, art, science, rhetoric, human philosophy—all were eliminated from early Christian education; and subjects quite foreign to the later pagan schools, moral and religious training, took their place. (p. Elmer Harrison Wilds, 160 from Kienel 3)

It is interesting and sad to note the similarities between our current public schools and those of pagan Rome and elsewhere.

All the schools were pagan. Not only were all the ceremonies of the official faith ... celebrated at regular intervals in the schools, but the children were taught reading out of books saturated with the old mythology. There the Christian child made the first acquaintance with the deities of Olympus. He ran the danger of imbibing ideas entirely contrary to those which he had received at home. The fables he had learned to detest in his own home were explained, elucidated, and held up to his admiration every day by his masters. Was it right to put him thus into two schools of thought? (quote 16, 8 of Kienel from 4 of Kienel)

Christian parents today understand the depth of intensity in the battle for their child's mind and soul. Paul Kienel writes,

For most early church Christians the choice was obvious. They would form their own schools. Nearly two thousand years later, Christian parents around the world are faced with the same dilemma—with one important difference. Paganism in non-Christian schools today is far less obvious than it was in Rome in A.D. 100. (Kienel 4)

Christian parents are choosing in increasing numbers to no longer allow their children to become part of the great public school experiment. Instead, Christian parents today are adopting a similar approach taken by Christian parents in the first century.

Increasingly, opposition grew to the worldly, pagan culture of the Greco-Roman world. On one hand, distinctly Christian schools began to develop; on the other, many Christians withdrew from Roman schools.

*A new tradition, of Christian schooling, dates from these early centuries after the birth of Christ.... In part, it was the tradition of **lectio divinia**; the centrality of reading the Holy Scriptures, reflecting that aspect of Christianity's origins that stressed the word as written and building on the Greek and Roman achievements in alphabetic literacy and in its popular dissemination. At the heart of this impulse was the inseparable connection of schooling with morality, which constitutes a major legacy.* (quote 26 p. 8 Kienel)

A Christian school history quickly moves from the first century and the early church fathers to the Puritans and the settlement of early America. The outgrowth of centuries of religious persecution, wars, and infighting within the Christian communities of Europe eventuated in an exodus of the persecuted religious to the new world. This purifying movement would lead to the establishment of Christianity on a brand new continent. The foundations for our present Christian school movement can be seen in the century by century focus on Christian schooling here on the North American continent.

In the 1600s American education was fundamentally Christian in nature. Students were taught to read to ensure their salvation. The thinking was if people could read the Bible, salvation was inevitable. The Puritans were arguably the most significant spiritual force in colonial America. During this time John Calvin became the spiritual father of America.

In the 1700s American education became a means to develop citizenship and homogenize the culture into a singular political force. The shift in educational philosophy moves from faith to reason and rationalism. The reformation with Luther, Bacon, Locke, Newton, Descartes, and many others leads the shift from nurture to nature, and God slowly becomes less significant in American education. In America, the Great Awakening, lead by Jonathan Edwards and his "Sinners in the Hands of an Angry God" sermon, helped to revive the spiritual focus of the new colonies.

In the 1800s American education developed an activist approach to educating the new country's youth. American education is transformed into a tool for social adjustment. In short, it becomes a propaganda tool for socialists, humanists, and the liberal elites. In 1805 Harvard is overrun by the Unitarians, which then lead to perhaps the foremost intellectual event of American education up to that point. The goal of the reformers was simply to get rid of Christianity, have schools become beautiful temples of man's glory, develop a national system of schools, and focus on rational training as the only means for educating youth.

In the 1900s American education comes full circle and is once again religious. However, the religion is now humanism. The progressivism of the late 1880s along with Darwin's work, and John Dewey's influence sets the stage for a philosophic overhaul of the American education establishment as radical as it was bold. Later, Freud, Piaget, Skinner, and many others infiltrate the educational machinery further propagating the humanist worldview of changing society and eventually changing the politics as well.

A Classic Excellence

The early 2000s have been very much impacted by the legislation from previous centuries. Examples of this educational shift from a legislative perspective include:

- 1642 MA, — Passes the first compulsory Education Law in the U.S.
- 1647 MA — Old Deluder Satan Act calls for establishment of schools
- 1779 VA, — Passes Jefferson's General Diffusion of Knowledge Bill
- 1784 NY, — Legislation passes funds to establish state academy
- 1785, NY, — Ordinance for rectangular survey of territories
- 1785, NY, — One-sixteenth section of new territories set aside for schools
- 1821, MA, — Boston establishes first public schools in U.S.
- 1834, PA, — Pennsylvania Free School Act
- 1837, MA, — Launches public school system
- 1862 Homestead Act — Provides money for acreage
- 1862 Morrow Act — Provides for land grant colleges
- 1878, *Reynolds v. U.S.* — Actions and beliefs need constitutional protection
- 1892, *Plessey v. Ferguson* — Separate but equal
- 1899, *Bradford v. Roberts* — Federal monies can go to Catholic schools
- 1923, *Mayer v. Nebraska* — Parents have right to send children to private school
- 1925, *Pierce v. Society of the Sisters of the Holy Names of Jesus and Mary* — Children must be raised in light of the high calling and in an effective manner
- 1930, *Cochran v. Louisiana* — Secular texts can be purchased with public funds for public schools

- 1940, *Cantrell v. Connecticut* Freedom of Jehovah's Witnesses to come into a town and distribute literature
- 1962, *Engle v. Vitale* Public prayer taken from schools, no precedent
- 1963, *Abington Township v. Schempp* Reading of Bible ruled unconstitutional in public schools
- 1965, ESEA First public funding for schools nationwide
- 1980, *State of Ohio v. Whisner* Ohio minimum standards requirement

In modern America, humanism has taken firm root. Humanism is now the basis for American public education. It is distinguished by the concept that wisdom and self-sufficiency is man-made, and that man has it all within himself to discover and manage life around him. It develops a self-worship or worship of man focus. It believes morals and values must be developed, and that they are not absolute. Humanism focuses on the emphasis of the present over the traditions of the past or the expectation and stewardship of the future. Is it any wonder God has called Christian schools to the necessary pursuit of excellence "for such a time as this"?

CHAPTER
one

Basic Excellence

> Now the Lord came and stood and called as at other times, "Samuel! Samuel!" And Samuel answered, "Speak, for Your servant hears."
>
> 1 Samuel 3:10

THE CALL

"Lord, I'm in sandals ... no socks, tattered shorts, stinky shirt. But I'll walk over there if you want me to." I was clearly having a difficult time believing what I was sensing. God was up to something big in my life. Like Samuel, and later David, God called me when I was "lying down." That is, I was neither looking, nor prepared to enter the ministry. In hindsight it was probably the only way I could have recognized His voice.

I had returned from traveling the world. North America, Europe, North Africa, Australia and the Far East sandwiched between owning a couple of pizza stores and earning a Masters in Education from Pepperdine University. Life's questions flowed through my very soul: What is truth? Why am I here? What am I supposed to be doing? Is there a heaven and hell?

Loneliness, despair, emptiness, and depression were my constant traveling companions. I had hoped that the busier I could make myself, the better chance I had of outrunning the utter wastefulness of life as I knew it. Pride in self-sufficiency, and a total lack of humility were like boulders strapped onto the sides of my backpack.

One fall I entered a graduate program in a small New England college. I knew it was forced, but I needed to keep moving. I quit after the first month. Shame and hopelessness shrouded my life like the impending New England winter. I was spiraling downward in rapid fashion.

Throwing myself at drugs and alcohol seemed to dull the sense of foreboding for a spell. I couldn't believe how far a person could fall in so short a time. I was a mess and needed a drastic overhaul in my heart, mind, and soul. One day a young man crossed my path in a weight room and changed my life forever.

The last day on campus before my lease was up, a young man with clear eyes and a ready smile told me of a place called L'Abri. It was a place to work half a day, study and investigate truth for half a day, eat three meals, and sleep. It was also a Christian ministry for skeptics like me, who just couldn't believe Christianity was the real deal. I stayed there until they closed the place for Christmas holiday.

One night prior to leaving L'Abri, during a bitter fall night, I gave my heart to Jesus. My simple prayer was, "God if You're there I'm here. I'm ready and I believe in Jesus as my Savior and I believe in You." My feet were chilled to the bone that night as they hung over the small wire cot. Frigid breezes stabbed at me through the eighteenth century wooden floorboards. After my prayer, the only thing warm was my chest that seemed to glow ever so slightly, as if touched by the flicker of a single matchstick.

Pride had precluded my acceptance of Christ. However, the witness of sincere Christians sparked a new interest in the truth of the identity of Jesus. The overwhelming evidence of Jesus afforded me the opportunity of a second chance. God is all about second chances. It was a simple lesson to learn.

Graduate school burnout, disillusionment with the teaching profession, and horror at the teachers' union led me to question my life's call. Likewise, a complete disagreement with the NEA and its philosophy led me to return to business ... two businesses, actually. Both failed.

It was during this "lying down" period when I was supple and still in the hands of the Master Potter, that God clarified His call for my life. First, I went to my church to purchase a devotional (I needed all the help I could get) and was intercepted by a frantic coach looking for someone to referee a junior high school flag football game, which was already some forty-five minutes late in starting. I recognized that both my businesses were closing down. All I had was time. Sure, I would help.

It went so well (How can you argue with a referee working for free?) I was asked to help with the next three games. My freshly minted degree and credentials qualified me to also pick up a stray PE class that met daily after lunch. Since the businesses were neatly closed out, I figured I could chalk the experience up to serving God somehow. I was now sensing God doing something special in my life.

Later, in natural progression, I picked up coaching duties for the junior high basketball team and three more classes. I was placed on payroll. I attended faculty meetings that opened in prayer. The school was sixty students and growing. There was a sense of wonder.

Increasingly, I was given more responsibility. I had been serving as Athletic Director for about six weeks. Our principal, a doctor in education and chair of the local State University Education Department, broke the news at one of our faculty meetings: he would not return as administrator next year. The search to replace him would be a national search. Something else happened at that meeting.

The Bible tells us, "Commit your works to the Lord, and your thoughts will be established" (Proverbs 16:3). The second our administrator told us he was not returning, a tingle went through my body. For the first time, a thought entered my mind. I felt like the little train in the children's fable who, when faced with climbing the big hill, said, "I think I can, I think I can."

One day, in shorts and sandals, I walked past our administrators' office. I was generally unfocused. Approximately twenty feet from his door I was stopped cold in my tracks by a deep impression in my spirit. I sensed I was to pray to be the next principal and to turn around and walk past—not go in—just walk past the office door. I was praying in abbreviated chitchat with the Lord at this point. I considered the importance of proper hygiene and the need for professional attire, and suggested such to the Lord. Not sensing an audible retort from Him, I haltingly obeyed and passed by the office door.

The administrator yelled my name as I passed, "Chapin!" My head turned on a swivel and I neatly poked only my head in his doorjamb, carefully concealing my grungy torso in a twisted, angular pose. He cupped the phone, caught his breath, and exclaimed that the pastor had asked if there was a young Samuel or David on staff that God would raise up to lead the school. He encouraged me to begin praying to that end. I told him I just had. He shook my hand and pulled me all the way into his office. "Great sandals," he exclaimed, "I've got a pair just like 'em."

In April I was named principal of the school. I had begun as a volunteer referee in October. The previous administrator left me this wisdom: "Where God guides, God provides." He told me to "trust God with everything and in everything trust God." I thanked him for the really, really great wisdom. I just had no idea what any of it meant.

I was waiting for direction, from anyone really; none arrived that day or the next. But a well-intentioned assistant pastor stopped by to share the ministry philosophy with me. "We don't have meetings, don't do memos, and if anyone needs to get plugged in to what's happening they just check in with the Holy Spirit." I was grateful for the guidance and all I could think was "huh?"

God's call, a specific appointment from God to you and me, is the first and most important requirement in serving in a Christian school. With the assurance of God's call comes peace. Without the assurance of God's call doubt can come, and fear and hopelessness. God's call on your life may be an encouragement in the lives of others.

One year the principal at our Christian school was without a high school English teacher, math teacher, and middle school science teacher. Not altogether remarkable except that school started on Tuesday and we were breaking for Labor Day weekend without the positions filled. One parent came to school the week prior to Labor Day and insisted the principal fill the positions or else she would pull her child from the school. The atmosphere with some parents became very tense.

Our principal continued to pray. He shared the prayer requests with his church. He waited. When the pressure had built and the line had been drawn in the sand, God moved. He quickened the heart of an English teacher, who had applied to our school the previous year when we had no openings, to do so again. God brought a math teacher from our parent ranks that not only had a teaching degree in math, but a master's degree in counseling from a world renowned university.

Then, God provided the coup de grâce. He had a science teacher from the Midwest call us after much prayer, to ask if we had any openings. Our principal had called weeks before. The science teacher had sensed God's call away from his current ministry. That July, in faith, he gave notice of his impending departure. He also notified his landlord he would be leaving at month's end. Then came the call from our principal. He told our principal he believed God had called him to our school. We agreed.

Our principal asked if he could make it to our school within the next few weeks. We believed we could arrange for a long-term sub. The science teacher told our principal his car was already packed. It was the last day on his lease. He had trusted God to send him somewhere. He was simply waiting for confirmation, and our phone call prior to driving over fifteen hundred miles to a new school, sight unseen.

God's call can be like that. It can be scary, unsettling, specific, personal, and ultimately supernatural. It is critical each of us obey His call upon our lives. If we choose to ignore it, or panic in the midst of His call, we may lose the blessing. The parent who complained about her child not having a teacher did request we send transcripts to a new school. We received the request within two hours of hiring the science teacher, our last academic course opening.

That parent could have grown in her faith. She could have discipled her child in the area of prayer, fasting, and faithfulness. Both the high qualifications and tender heart to serve Christ that all three new teachers offered would have blessed her. Alas, she missed a God-given opportunity to be blessed by the process of His hand at work.

The need for excellence in Christian schools is acute. We need to live our lives by faith. Our ministries should be faith factories. The reason is simple, "But without faith it is impossible to please Him" (Hebrews 11:6). The next generation Christian school is excellence-oriented, faith-focused, not ashamed of the gospel, and Christ-centered. The need for this simple, yet radical approach to a classic excellence in our Christian schools is long overdue. In the end, it is our call. Each of us, in every ministry, needs to consider our call.

The Need

I discovered how little I understood about Christian education when I was called into my first principal position. Quickly, I called around to seek help. Christian schools, once growing past their founders' expectations, had lost the freshness originally breathed by God. Administrative vision had, in many cases, grown old, tired, or ineffectual. Old mimeograph machines or outdated Xerox copiers ran off barely legible operational forms. Some schools had only oral policies. The smell in some of the schools was a musty, moldy, stagnant smell of complacency. I was scared.

Dozens of Christian schools were located in basements, sanctuary overflow rooms, and undersized warehouses. It occurred to me that the first Christians must have started something like this. The original church was like the Christian school movement. It was courageous, vibrant, focused, and full of great vision. What happened? Why were Christian schools still in the "basement"?

In so many Christian schools an unmistakable love for God and His children is evident. In most of the schools I visited, I witnessed a strong commitment to Christian education, as well. Something was wrong, though, in too many of these original works of God. What happened? Something was missing.

Joy was conspicuously absent. We can easily slip away from keeping Jesus as the core of all we do. Much like Mary and Joseph, we can be living, even fellowshipping with Jesus, and then subtly over time we have lost Him. Stopping, we turn to look where we've lost Him. We run quickly to the town, as Mary and Joseph did, only to find Him about "His Father's business." Jesus was in the temple preparing for His ministry.

Christian ministry can be deceptively unspiritual. Quick prayer early in the morning, the obligatory ten-minute devotional and we're out the door to "run the ministry." Relationships with others in our Christian schools can be strained when we operate our schools by the wisdom of the world. Our focus of Jesus can be subtly lost in the duties of the day.

In many cases, Christian schools lack a clear, updated vision for ministry. The Bible tells us that "without a vision the people perish" (Proverbs 29:18). Too many Christian schools are dying on the vine. Everyone in the school family suffers when the vision has died. This is sad.

Christian schools, in a general sense, lack recognizable quality. For example, quality is lost on teacher selection. To be sure, low pay and minimal benefits play a part in teacher selection. Likewise, Christian school boards could do more to establish higher standards for teacher selection. Creative pay structures could also be developed to meet the needs of those willing to sacrifice financially to teach at Christian schools. Some ideas include flextime schedules, endowments to support continuing education, and sabbaticals for research and spiritual refreshment.

Parent organizations within the school could provide monies for individual and group retreats, surprise vacations, and the like. One East Coast school's parent group sends out a list to parents of each child's teachers, the administrative team over the child, and the secretaries and support staff. At Christmastime the parents give a little money and designate a portion to whomever they wish to bless. Prior to Christmas break, the faculty and staff receive, in some instances, hundreds of dollars from parents wishing to bless them. It is a wonderful tool to show appreciation and the love of God toward one another.

In the end, ministry is a faith walk. Christian parents sacrifice to send their children to these schools. But should they do so on the backs of teachers who are paid less than a babysitter? We can do better. We must do better. The future of our children is at stake. Christian educators should be paid a reasonable living wage. The $14,000 or $16,000 we currently start so many of our new teachers at is, in most regions of the country, laughable.

Textbook selection is another area of concern in Christian education. Frankly, the largest Christian publishers need to pay more attention to accuracy rather than to grinding their respective theological axes. In too many instances Christian schools cannot, in good faith, order Christian texts because the information is either grossly outdated, inaccurate, or fiercely denominational. Christian textbook publishing is over a $1 billion per year industry/ministry. Surely we can do better.

Unfortunately, there also tends to be lack of meaningful offerings throughout the curriculum at most Christian schools. Some ideas to diversify offerings include work-study and vocational-technical programs in partnership with larger Christian schools and the local community college programs. Partnerships with area home-school groups can be a great source of synergies for a common cause. Also, Christian schools can, after prayer and the leading of the Lord, step out in faith and start enrichment, remediation, honors, and advanced placement programs. Christian schools need distinctives across the board to set us apart. God deserves the best. Why do we limit Him?

It took me over ten years of administrating and consulting Christian schools to see that the Lord wants to do more. The familiar refrain of, "We're a ministry" so often used to excuse away mediocre pay, marginal texts, minimal extracurricular activities, and the like, must be expunged from our collective mindsets. It has been said, "Our expectations are our only limitations." Administrating, teaching, and supporting a Christian school is a calling from God. Inspired dreamers waiting for God's call and direction are now needed. Come, let us dream together. God's will in you is His will for you.

The Fruit: Friendship With God

Most every Christian would agree with the statement "I want to do God's will." I am certain most of us would shy away from arguing against this notion. The next step, then, is to discover what that really means. What is it to truly know God's will for our lives? Though hundreds of books have been written on the subject, included here is a simple yet practical approach to the very question of God's will in our lives. Once we understand better God's will in our lives, we are then better positioned to fulfill the needs He places in front of us each and every day.

In his work *My Utmost for His Highest*, Oswald Chambers speaks wonderfully on the idea of God's will in the life of the Christian. God delights in His children. The Lord loves to lead us in "paths of righteousness for His name's sake." God's delight in us is reflected in Scripture.

Shall I hide from Abraham what I am doing?

Genesis 18:17

Delights

This chapter brings out the delight of real friendship with God as compared with occasional feelings of His presence in prayer. To be so much in contact with God that you never need to ask Him to show you His will, is to be nearing the final stage of your discipline in the life of faith. When you are rightly related to God, it is a life of freedom and liberty and delight; you *are* God's will, and all your common sense decisions are His will for you unless He checks. You decide things in perfectly delightful friendship with God, knowing that if your decisions are wrong He will always check; and when He checks, stop at once.

Difficulties

Why did Abraham stop praying when he did? He was not intimate enough yet to go boldly on until God granted his desire—there was something yet to be desired in his relationship with God. Whenever we stop short in prayer and say, "Well, I don't know, perhaps it is not God's will," there is still another stage to go. We are not so intimately acquainted with God as Jesus was, and as He wants us to be, "That they may be one as we are" (John 17:11). Think of the last thing you prayed about—were you devoted to your desire or to God? Determined to get some gift of the Spirit or to get at God? "For your Heavenly Father knows that you need all these things" (Matthew 6:32). The point of asking is that you may get to know God better. "Delight yourself also in the Lord, And He shall give you the desires of your heart." Keep praying in order to get perfect understanding of God Himself."

Often I find in my own life that it is not so much understanding God's call for me or our school, as it is being obedient to Him. Like Peter, I may tend to be presumptuous or impetuous. Often God simply requires us to wait. In most cases a thorough evaluation of our circumstances and prayer to the Father will sort things out for His glory and our benefit. Here are twelve questions to ask to know God's will for our lives and our ministries. This is taken from "Silent Strength for My Life," by Lloyd John Ogilvie.

He who does the will of God abides forever.

1 John 2:17

Here are twelve questions to ask and answer in a practical inventory for making a maximized decision under the Lord's guidance:

1. Is it consistent with the Ten Commandments?
2. Will it deepen my relationship with Christ?
3. Is it an extension of Christ's life, message, and kingdom?
4. If I do it, will it glorify Him and enable me to grow as His disciple?
5. Is there a scriptural basis for it?
6. Is it adventuresome enough to need the Lord's presence and power to accomplish it?
7. Has prolonged prayer and thought produced an inner feeling of "rightness" about it?
8. Is it something for which I can praise Him in advance of doing or receiving it?
9. Is it an expression of authentic love, and will it bring ultimate good in the lives of the people involved?
10. Will it be consistent with my basic purpose to love the Lord and be a communicator of His love to others?
11. Will it enable me to grow in the talents and gifts the Lord has given me?

12. Will my expenditures still allow tithing plus generous giving of my money for the Lord's work and the needs of others?

These questions I ask. There are many things I have not done because I could not say yes to all twelve of these. Of course, when I look back, the poorest choices and decisions have been made when I didn't ask or answer all of them. But the Lord gives forgiveness and the challenge, "Tomorrow's another day, another chance, and a new beginning" (226).

A Classic Excellence is a book about Jesus. It happens to be told against the backdrop of Christian education. Make no mistake about it though, Jesus is the reason for this book. God's call to start and operate a Christian school is the only reason to do so. God called His only Son into a ministry to redeem and transform lives. That is the sole aim of Christian education.

THE CHALLENGE: STARTING A CHRISTIAN SCHOOL

There are three simple steps to starting a Christian school. The questions to be asked before starting a Christian school are:

1. Is God breathing a Christian school into existence?
   If so …
2. Is God calling YOU to help start a Christian school?
   If so …
3. Are YOU and others willing to OBEY the CALL of God?

There are ample resources for those interested in the specifics of starting a Christian school. These resources include timetables, development schedules, boilerplate policy and procedure forms, job descriptions, and much more. Three resources to consider in starting a Christian school would include:

1. Association of Christian Schools International, (ACSI) *Starting a New Christian School-Operations Manual.* Available through ACSI at P.O. Box 35097, Colorado Springs, CO 80935-3509. Phone # (719) 528-1201.

ACSI also has wonderful resources dealing with finance, board relations, supervision, instruction, and much more.

2. DEL Publications, *Christian Schools, How to Get a School Going and Keep It Growing,* Del Publishers, 5747 South Utica, Suite 101, Tulsa, OK 74105-8038. Phone # (918) 749-2157

3. A Beka Book, *The Successful Christian School,* A Beka Book Publishers, Pensacola Christian College, Pensacola, Florida 32523-91.

CHAPTER

two

Just Jesus

Jesus said, "Let the little children come to Me, and do not forbid them; for of such is the kingdom of God. Assuredly, I say to you, whoever does not receive the kingdom of God as a little child will by no means enter it." And He took them up in His arms, laid His hands on them, and blessed them.

Mark 10:14–16

THE PASSION

"You are a Christian, aren't you?" my pastor asked me. "Yes I am," I replied nervously. He was silent for an interminable moment. Tilting his head to the left and raising an eyebrow, a dead giveaway that my pastor already knew my answer, he quietly asked, "You love kids, right?" Like a bridegroom at the altar I smiled, "I do." So began the call of a lifetime. God called me into the ministry of Christian education with two simple questions: "Do you love me?" and "Do you love kids?"

Our pastor had need of a Christian school principal. He prayed that God would fill that need. He waited. I prayed that God would use me to the fullest for His glory. I waited. God is never late and rarely early. His timing is not for us to understand, but if we truly place our trust in Him, we find that

His timing is perfect. In waiting, I learned my responsibility is to listen, pray, and obey.

THE RESPONSE

The Waiting Game: Lessons Learned While Waiting with God

"I'm waiting!" Finally, somewhat exasperated I groaned to God these words: "I'm waiting over here!" I'd prayed, fasted, repented, read His Word, scoured devotionals, sat still (hated it), sought godly counsel, and still I was waiting. Anybody else been there, done that? Here is an insight I pray might encourage you in God's waiting room.

Gideon waiting on the fleece to confirm the call (Judges 6–8)

Do you know that someone is praying for you right now? That's right. Someone far away or perhaps right next door, is praying for the gifts and skills God has equipped you with. You see, the need in their ministry is clear. The people are beseeching God to bring someone to help. You are that someone. They are waiting for you to hear God's call, to go and minister your gifts to their need.

Judges chapters 6 and 7 say, "And it came to pass, when the children of Israel cried out to the Lord because of the Midianites, that the Lord sent a prophet to the children of Israel." This prophet reminded Israel of God's faithfulness and their disobedience. Next, God sent an angel to the man chosen of God to minister to the needs of the children of Israel. The first words to God's chosen man, Gideon, were words of encouragement. "The Lord is with you, you mighty man of valor" (Judges 6:12).

The angel found Gideon threshing wheat in the winepress

in order to hide it from the Midianites. Gideon was in a time of withdrawal. He was not exercising his highest giftedness for God's glory. In fact he was hiding from God's call, and from life's great adventure. What was oppressive was expected. Fear was his constant tormentor. What he had experienced as numbness seemed normal.

God's called need never be fearful. God's call brings life and is not oppressive, bland, boring or discouraging. Gideon had his focus on his circumstances, not on his God. His glance *bleppo* was on God, but his gaze *skopio* was on his circumstance. Any time we glance at God and gaze at the world, we are in trouble. Our entire focus must be a continual gaze at God and His will. Then as we glance briefly at life's circumstances, will we get clarity of vision and victory in action through prayer and God's Word.

Gideon was so focused on his immediate circumstance that as God was calling him, Gideon's waiting was a function of his wavering. First, he asked Angel of the Lord, "O my lord, if the Lord is with us, why then has all this happened to us? And where are all His miracles which our fathers told us about . . . ?" Gideon didn't realize that he, like you or me, was about to be used by God as a living miracle. Sometimes our gaze limits our vision. God or circumstances—what do you choose to focus on?

Gideon complained that "my clan is the weakest in Manasseh, and I am the least in my father's house." When God calls us we need to keep our eye on the ball. We need to remember to separate ourselves from the things that separate us from God. This includes family, friends, expectations, traditions, and the like. We need to be ready to do things God's way and to be obedient to God's Word. Finally, don't forget what God has done and is doing in our lives.

The "gifts and the calling of God are irrevocable" (Romans

11–29). What we choose to do with our gifts and calling are exactly that, a choice. God told Gideon "Surely I will be with you, and you shall defeat the Midianites as one man" (Judges 6:16). That promise is for us today too. Will we choose to believe God at His word? Gideon didn't. His response was that if God were serious, "then (He would) show me a sign" (Judges 6:17). Later, "Gideon said to God, 'If You will save Israel by my hand as You have said, look, I shall put a fleece of wool on the threshing floor; if there is dew on the fleece only, and it is dry on all the ground, then I shall know that You will save Israel by my hand, as You have said'" (Judges 6:36–37).

The Israelites were waiting on Gideon. Likewise, people are waiting on you and me as we wait on God for an answer. He may already have given us the answer. Sometimes we wait because our faith is weak. *We wonder, What if I obey and things don't work out?* Other times we doubt we are hearing God at all. God's voice never condemns, though the Holy Spirit does convict. God's voice does not discourage, though He does challenge. God's voice brings expectancy, not anxiety. Gideon, after all this waiting, still had to reverse his fleece test one more time to get it absolutely clear in his mind that it was indeed a call of God. All the while people were praying and waiting for God to deliver them by a miracle. Gideon and his army were that miracle. God uses people just like you and me.

Gideon finally answered the call. For him, the waiting must have been extreme. Think about it for a moment. His people are in bondage; God calls Gideon to save the people. At some point he realizes he really is God's man. A crisis of belief ensues; he can obey or disobey. It is a scary thought because after saying yes to God, the next question is how to fulfill God's call.

Imagine, for a moment, God calling us to begin a building project. We finally agree to lead the enterprise. Right away we assess the situation and find we have $320,000. We need ten times that amount, but we have a good start, sort of. You see, God tells us to give $220,000 back to donors if they don't want to stay with the project. In addition God says, as we are set to start, we are only allowed $3,000 to begin. The other $97,000 is to be given away. Like Gideon, we need to be humble and alert.

Immediately, we discover "'For My thoughts are not your thoughts, Nor are your ways My ways,' says the Lord." (Is 55:8) Through all of this Gideon is waiting. The Israelites are waiting as they cry to God for deliverance. The 300 chosen soldiers in Gideon's army are waiting as God forms their team. No question that doubt, fear, frustration, perhaps division and discord, entered in as God set the stage in Gideon's call for a God-sized miracle. The whole plan is counterintuitive to our natural way of doing things.

Gideon hears a dream and interpretation, an example of God using the gifts in the body to edify one another. He divides his troops, and gives every man a clay pitcher with a torch inside. Next, Gideon models a valuable lesson in leadership. "And he said to them, 'Look at me and do likewise; watch, and when I come to the edge of the camp you shall do as I do'" (Judges 7:17). God had asked Gideon to do the improbable in the midst of the impossible—to lead a small army against overwhelming odds.

Gideon's army used clay pots to confuse and surprise the Midianites. The clay pots held the most precious possessions in that day. The pots held valuables so robbers wouldn't be suspicious. The torches or light in the clay pots are like our lives, a symbol of the Holy Spirit in us. We are made of clay, broken and cracked to show the light of Christ's victory. Much like jewelers who use the blackest fabric as background to highlight the most expensive diamond, God uses you and me to reveal His glory to a lost and dying world today. It may be time for you and me to come out of withdrawal. Jesus is either Lord of all or not Lord at all.

The pitchers were broken, torches raised, trumpets blown, the Midianites were devastated and captured. The power of God through Gideon's faith overwhelmed the Midianites. As Gideon was faithful, the fullness of God's supernatural power and wisdom was unleashed through Gideon's army on behalf of the Israelites. The long wait was finally over. Like Gideon, God has called you and me to a faith walk. In exercising our faith in accordance with God's will, we will experience miracles, that is, supernatural stuff. Remember, the Lord is with you mighty man of valor! (Judges 6:12)

THE PURPOSE

Two years later I was called out of a very important board meeting with the words, "Mr. Marsh, we need your help." The meeting topics were intense and the agenda was demanding. In unison we stared at the partially opened door. Through that door the partially disembodied floating hand of my secretary, waved the note through the air which read: "Mr. Marsh, we need your help *now*!"

My first thoughts were along the lines of, "Can't you deal with it?" My secretary clearly knew this was a critical meeting; nothing could be so important that I should be called out. I put on an appropriate "angry-principal" frown and silently harrumphed across the campus with secretary in tow not saying a single word. Her job was to free me up to deal with the really important stuff, or so I thought.

My next thoughts were equally pointed. *I am too busy for interruptions.* Stomping into the office I made enough noise for everyone to see my displeasure. *Swoosh*! A stack of papers flew to the ground. *Kaaplunk*! A book sternly moved from one corner of my desk to the other with no apparent advantage. "What's so important?" I barked to no one in particular. My secretary pointed just outside the office window.

The red headed boy whose hair had never been tamed by the comb was sitting on a long bench in front of my office. Students in trouble sat there. I braced myself for the worst. My typical prayer of "Dear God, please give me wisdom in this matter," preceded the confrontation. I recognized the boy immediately. It was AWOL Albert. He was a troubled child whose behavior at school had been marginal at best.

My secretary quickly informed me that, true to form, the young man was out of class without permission again. He had come to her office in tears, by now quite obvious. I was impatient, frustrated, and becoming angry. I was losing valuable time with the board. I stared at my secretary with pointed daggers and asked icily, "Is there anything more?"

Unfazed, she responded, "Yes, one more thing. He has asked for you specifically." She breathed the contented pause of a cat that has trapped a mouse in the corner and is now simply enjoying the game. "Sooo…" I said, more to be a nuisance than anything else. Her warm, composed glow gave away the blessing she called to share. "He wants to give his life to Jesus. I'll leave you two alone." The smile on her face was only surpassed by the kindness in her eyes. I was numb, humbled, and embarrassed. I sat down next to the boy. We talked about life, parents, Jesus and salvation for the next two hours. He accepted Jesus sometime during our time together. I couldn't tell you what the board discussed that day.

Interruptions are God's invitations. Children, parents, grandparents, and anyone in contact with the Christian school are divine appointments. We must never allow the business of a day's work to interrupt the timing of God's plan. Knowing Jesus personally is a prerequisite for effective Christian school ministry. Choosing to love people is the fundamental purpose of the Christian school ministry.

What masquerades as an interruption is really an invitation to get involved in the life of someone deeply loved by God. In fact, on some level God has sent them to you and to me because He feels there is a chance we will be faithful to share Jesus and His love to those He sends through our ministries. People are the priority. Stuff can wait.

The lesson I learned that day helped me refocus, back to my heart's original purpose: to love children and lead them to Christ. In two short years, the cares of the world had already choked out my passion. The excellence we pursue must always focus on God's eternal purpose. Eternal excellence begins and ends with love. Jesus said, "Love one another as I have loved you" (John 15:12).

Love is a choice. Accepting Jesus as Savior is a choice. Keeping Jesus as the most important thing in the ministry is a choice. The following story was passed along to me in an e-mail from my friend Bob Johnson. It underscores the subtle yet powerful importance of keeping Jesus as the primary focus of the Christian school ministry.

A wealthy man and his son loved to collect rare works of art. They had everything in their collection, from Picasso to Raphael. They would often sit together and admire the great works of art.

When the Viet Nam conflict broke out, the son went to war. He was very courageous and died in battle while rescuing another soldier.

The father was notified and grieved deeply for his only son. About a month later, just before Christmas, there was a knock at the door. A young man stood at the door with a large package in his hands. He said, "Sir, you don't know me, but I am the soldier for whom your son gave his life. He saved many lives that day, and he was carrying me to safety when a bullet struck him in the heart and he died instantly. He often talked about you, and your love for art." The young man held out his package. "I know this isn't much. I'm not really a great artist, but I think your son would have wanted you to have this."

The father opened the package. It was a portrait of his son, painted by the young man. He stared in awe at the way the soldier had captured the personality of his son in the painting. The father was so drawn to the eyes that his own welled up with tears.

He thanked the young man and offered to pay for the picture. "Oh, no sir, I could never repay what your son did for me. It's a gift."

The father hung the portrait over his mantle. Every time visitors came to his home, he took them to see the portrait of his son before he showed them any of the other great works he had collected.

The man died a few months later. There was to be a great auction of his paintings. Many influential people gathered, excited to seeing the great paintings and to have an opportunity to purchase one for their collection.

On the platform sat the painting of the son. The auctioneer pounded his gavel. "We will start the bidding with this picture of the son. Who will bid for this picture?"

There was silence. Then a voice in the back of the room shouted: "We want to see the famous paintings. Skip this one."

But the auctioneer persisted. "Will someone bid for this painting? Who will start the bidding? $100? $200?"

Another voice shouted angrily. "We didn't come to see this painting. We came to see the Van Goghs, the Rembrandts. Get on with the real bids!"

But still the auctioneer continued. "The son! The son! Who'll take the son?"

Finally, a voice came from the very back of the room. It was the long-time gardener of the man and his son. "I'll give ten dollars for the painting."

Being a poor man, it was all he could afford.

"We have ten dollars, who will bid twenty dollars?"

"Give it to him for ten dollars. Let's see the masters!"

"Ten dollars is the bid. Won't someone bid twenty dollars?"

The crowd was becoming angry. They didn't want the picture of the son. They wanted the more worthy investments for their collections.

The auctioneer pounded the gavel. "I'm sorry, the auction is over."

"What about the paintings?"

"I am sorry. When I was called to conduct this auction, I was told of a secret stipulation in the will. I was not allowed to reveal that stipulation until this time. Only the painting of the son would be auctioned. Whoever bought that painting would inherit the entire estate, including the paintings. The man who took the son gets everything!"

God sent His only Son 2,000 years ago to die on a cruel cross. Much like the auctioneer, His message today is "The Son, the Son, who'll take the Son?"

Because, you see, whoever takes the Son gets everything.

"For the gifts and the calling of God are irrevocable" (Romans 11:29). Ministry can be grueling work. Sometimes it can feel like ditch digging along the Panama Canal or towing a barge by your teeth while swimming the English Channel.

It is often difficult to stay passionate about God in the midst of trials, temptations, and the daily grind. Jesus, just Jesus, is the only hope we have as we pursue God's purposes for excellence in Christian education. God's specific call is the only reason to start and operate a Christian school.

THE PROTECTION

I was shocked! A pastor from a local church in town had just spent the last two and a half hours telling me how I had mishandled every aspect of his son's discipline. The good pastor's wife was equally pointed in her personal attacks. I was numb! I wanted to cry. I was too angry to reply. I listened, angry, frustrated, hurt, and shocked.

The young man, a junior in our high school, had been teasing and tempting other students to join him in some truly hellish behavior. In short order, this young man offered alcohol, drugs, and sex to students in our school. The coup de grâce was a pentagram he wrote on the ground in front of his math room. His math teacher caught him in the very act. She promptly prayed for him, prayed over the ground, and reported him to the office.

In each instance there was firsthand, eyewitness evidence. Concerning alcohol and drugs, students voluntarily alerted us that this young man had solicited them. Pertaining to overt sexual advances, young men conflicted and confused, shared that he had touched their shoulders and back and offered to do more. In one case the threat of physical violence accompanied the unwanted advances. The last straw was the pentagram.

The boy's parents stormed into my office with such force that I felt it necessary to scoop off my desk any items that could have become projectiles aimed at me. "I suppose you have never made a mistake, Mr. Marsh!" the mother intoned.

"Where is the grace? Jesus came to set people like you and me free. People like my son. Don't forget the story of the woman at the well!" she continued.

Her razor sharp gaze knifed toward her husband. "Did *you* see my son do any of these things?" he accused. "As I mentioned …" I began, but he cut me off. "I understand what you have told us. So you are telling me you are taking the word of one student over another? You believe a teacher who we know does not like my son. You believe her? Is that what you are telling us?" His voice was so loud and booming it sent shock ripples in concentric circles throughout my coffee. Waves literally appeared.

Silence. Recognizing that after more than two hours, nothing I could say would improve things, I said nothing. Silence. Hard, angry, bitter stares in silence.

"Mr. Marsh, you are the worst example of a Christian I have ever seen," the Mrs. interjected. "*Are* you a Christian?" She placed the emphasis on *Are* this time. "Yes, ma'am, I am," I offered. "Don't you dare get sarcastic with my wife, son. You can be assured I will report your complete bungling of this matter to the church, the school board, the pastor, and whoever else will listen. This whole affair is a disgrace."

Silently, I couldn't have agreed with him more. The pastor and his wife were having trouble recognizing that the sin nature in all of us was flaring up in their teenage son. The pride of being embarrassed by his behavior was ruling their lives. For my part, I held close to the Lord and the Scripture not to esteem one man higher than another. The lesson I learned in the midst of terrible attack was to do the right thing because it is the right thing to do. A couple of times I would have preferred to acquiesce and let the issue die. It wasn't the right thing to do though.

"I am sorry we ever enrolled our son in this awful school.

If this is the way a Christian school is run, our future is in jeopardy. You have damaged my son and caused great harm to our family. I am holding you personally responsible for the horrific manner in which this situation has been handled. You should be ashamed of yourself," the pastor concluded.

This type of personal attack did nothing but frustrate me further. I learned a long time ago to simply grin and bear it. Anything that I said at this point could and would be held against me. So, I spent my time under the inquisition staring at the strangely shaped alignment of moles on the woman's face and neck. I wondered if she realized how very much like a sonar grid her face looked when she became angry.

In the two and a half hours we were there, I also noticed eighteen moles on his face and neck. Did he know how red his face got when he stuttered in anger? Did he have any awareness how unattractive the white spittle dried in the corner of his mouth was? Did he know he had eighteen moles? Since the meeting was a harangue, and discussion from me was discouraged, I thought it would give a better impression if I nodded my head obliquely up and down as I counted. I counted three times for accuracy.

"I would like to pray for us if that would suit," I asked. "Ha!" the mother vomited. "Honey," the pastor interrupted, "praying can only help, even if it's from an incompetent. Please do pray for us, and while you're at it, search your heart for the sin that is causing others to hurt so much. We have spoken to a number of families who feel the job you are doing can best be described as inept. Trust me when I say you haven't heard the last from us. We will not stop until justice and fairness are served."

"Let's pray," I choked out.

Furious and hurt, I left that meeting with my stomach knotted up in pending rage. How had I become such a bad guy when all I did was my job? What was God trying to teach me in this situation? I was learning that consistency in all discipline was the key. I learned to execute what we implemented. I learned that God's call is greater than man's rage. For this young man we administrated discipline as per our school handbook.

This family's strong reaction to a simple case of sin in their son's life reflected a deeper set of expectations. Often the most difficult people to deal with are those already serving the Lord in ministry. In some instances those in ministry, especially in leadership, believe they are sacrificing enough already for the body of Christ. In some small way they believe they are entitled to preferential treatment. Often our only solace is to lick our wounds, give our hurts to the Lord, and pray for the people who have wronged or hurt us.

A dear friend of mine prayed with me. I saw no hope in the circumstance. Threatened and backed into a corner, I felt helpless and vulnerable. I no longer sensed God's powerful protection. It was a scary time.

My friend began to share a story of God's protection in the midst of perilous times. She shared how turmoil is used of God in each of our lives. God can use tragedy and turmoil to get us to a place of hearing His voice clearly. She shared her experience of finding that when it's least expected, God may be doing His greatest work in our lives and circumstances. I listened intently to her story.

A cold March wind danced around the dead of night in Dallas as the doctor walked into the small hospital room of Diana Blessing.

With her still feeling groggy from surgery, Diana's husband, David, held her hand as they braced themselves for the latest news. That afternoon of March 10, 1991, complications had forced Diana, only twenty-four weeks pregnant, to undergo an emergency cesarean to deliver the couple's new daughter, Danae Lu Blessing. At twelve inches long and weighing only one pound and nine ounces, they already knew she was perilously premature.

Still, the doctor's soft words dropped like bombs. "I don't think she's going to make it," he said, as kindly as he could. "There's only a 10 percent chance she will live through the night, and even then, if by some slim chance she does make it, her future could be a very cruel one."

Numb with disbelief, David and Diana listened as the doctor described the devastating problems Danae would likely face if she survived. She would never walk; she would never talk; she would probably be blind; she would certainly be prone to other catastrophic conditions from cerebral palsy to complete mental retardation, and on and on.

"No! No!" was all Diana could say. She and David, with their five-year-old son Dustin, had long dreamed of the day that they would have a little girl to become a family of four. Now, within a matter of hours, that dream was slipping away.

Through the dark hours of morning as Danae held onto life by the thinnest of threads, Diana slipped in and out of drugged sleep, growing more and more determined that their tiny daughter would live—and live to be a healthy, happy young girl. But David, fully awake and listening to additional dire details of their daughter's chances of ever leaving the hospital alive, much less healthy, knew he must confront his wife with the inevitable.

David walked in and told Diana that they needed to talk about making funeral arrangements. Diana remembers feeling so bad for him because he was doing everything and trying to include her in what was going on. She just wouldn't listen. She couldn't listen. She said, "No. That is not going to happen. No way! I don't care what the doctors say; Danae is not going to die! One day she will be just fine, and she will be coming home with us!"

As if willed to live by Diana's determination, Danae clung to life hour after hour, with the help of every medical machine and marvel her miniature body could endure. But as those first days passed, a new agony set in for David and Diana.

Because Danae's underdeveloped nervous system was essentially "raw" the lightest kiss or caress only intensified her discomfort. They couldn't ever cradle their tiny baby against their chests to offer the strength of their love. All they could do as Danae struggled alone beneath the ultraviolet light in the tangle of tubes and wires was to pray that God would stay close to their precious little girl.

As the weeks went by, she slowly gained an ounce of weight here and an ounce of strength there. At last, when Danae turned two months old, her parents were able to hold her in their arms for the very first time. Two months later, though doctors continued gently but grimly to warn that her chances of surviving, much less living any kind of normal life, were next to zero, Danae went home from the hospital, just as her mother had predicted.

Today, five years later, Danae is a petite but feisty young girl with glittering gray eyes and an unquenchable zest for life. She shows no signs whatsoever of any mental or physical impairments. Simply, she is everything a little girl can be, and more. But that happy ending is far from the end of her story.

One blistering afternoon in the summer of 1996 near her home in Irving, Texas, Danae was sitting in her mother's lap in the bleachers of a local ballpark where her brother Dustin's baseball team was practicing. As always, Danae was chattering nonstop with her mother and several other adults sitting nearby when she suddenly fell silent.

Hugging her arms across her chest, Danae asked, "Do you smell that?" Smelling the air and detecting an approaching thunderstorm, Diana replied, "Yes, it smells like rain." Danae closed her eyes and again asked, "Do you smell that?" Once again her mother replied, "Yes, I think we are about to get wet. It smells like rain." Still caught in the moment, Danae shook her head, patted her thin shoulders with her small hands and loudly announced, "No. It smells like Him. It smells like God when you lay your head on His chest."

Tears blurred Diana's eyes as Danae then happily hopped down to play with the other children. Before the rains came, her daughter's words confirmed what Diana and all the members of the extended Blessing family had known, at least in their hearts, all along. During those long days and nights of her first two months of life, when her nerves were too sensitive for them to touch her, God was holding Danae on His chest, and it is His loving scent that she remembers so well. God's protection had covered Danae's life. God had personally cared for and held Danae during that traumatic time of her life.

Through tear-soaked hands I was learning to trust that God's protection would cover my life as well. The incident with the parents who had so completely caught me off guard would be used of God in my life and ministry. At the time I couldn't put my finger on exactly why I had to go through it, but I knew it was for my best, "and that He might make known the riches of His glory on the vessels of mercy, which He had prepared beforehand for glory." (Romans 9:23)

The Provision

Prayer changes things. It is always best to wait for God's best. Prayer is the means to speak and to listen to God. It has been said that God gave us two ears and one mouth to direct us in how we should be spending the majority of our time with Him. God guides a ministry as He provides for it. His provision always begins with prayer.

In his booklet, *Things I Leaned from My Pastor*, Larry Taylor writes, "Prayer is not a means to convince God to give us what we want, it is a means by which we can participate in His will. It is the channel through which He works. Prayer moves the heart of God."[1] The passion, protection, and provision for Christian school ministry begins and ends in prayer. The Christian school grows from the knees up.

The following illustration, shared by our business manager Steve Adkins, addresses the power of prayer and the humility of leaning upon God's provision.

The weight of prayer

Louise Redden, a poorly dressed lady with a look of defeat on her face, walked into a grocery store. She approached the owner of the store in a most humble manner and asked if he would let her charge a few groceries.

She softly explained that her husband was very ill and unable to work, they had seven children and they needed food. John Longhouse, the grocer, scoffed at her and requested that she leave his store. Visualizing the family needs, she said, "Please, sir! I will bring you the money just as soon as I can."

John told her he could not give her credit, as she did not have a charge account at his store. Standing beside the counter was a customer who overheard the conversation between the two. The customer walked forward and told the grocer man that he would stand good for whatever she needed for her family. The grocer man said in a very reluctant voice, "Do you have a grocery list? Louise replied "Yes sir!"

"O.K." the grocer said: "Put your grocery list on the scales and whatever your grocery list weighs, I will give you that amount in groceries." Louise hesitated a moment with a bowed head, then she reached into her purse and took out a piece of paper and scribbled something on it. She then laid the piece of paper on the scale carefully with her head still bowed. The eyes of the grocer and the customer showed amazement when the scales went down and stayed down. The grocer staring at the scales turned slowly to the customer and said begrudgingly, "I can't believe it." The customer smiled,

and the grocer started putting the groceries on the other side of the scales. The scale did not balance, so he continued to put more and more groceries on them until the scales would hold no more. The grocer stood there in utter disgust. Finally, he grabbed the piece of paper from the scales and looked at it with greater amazement. It was not a grocery list; it was a prayer, which said: "Dear Lord, you know my needs and I am leaving this in your hands." The grocer gave her the groceries from off the scales and stood in stunned silence.

Louise thanked him and left the store. The customer handed a fifty-dollar bill to John, and he said, "it was worth every penny of it." Only later did John Longhouse discover the scales were broken. Therefore, only God knows how much a prayer weighs.

God also knows the weight of the burden to begin or to improve a Christian school. God places ideas, passion, and purpose deep within our souls as we pray. Our natural gifts and abilities swing into action. Prayer, humility, patience, and high expectations are hallmarks of the successful Christian school. God's passion, protection, and provision begin to vividly come to life in schools that are alive in faith.

The story of Dan Cook and Associates is one of passion, protection, and provision on a God-sized scale. In the town of Provo, Utah, in the early 1990s, Dan Cook sought a Christian school for his children to attend. Provo is a Mormon community of well over 70 percent practicing Mormons. Biblical Christianity is taboo in Provo. Practicing Christians are at a decided disadvantage.

Dan traveled around the country and discovered (much like I have) that Christian schools are building or leasing the wrong kinds of buildings to suit their purposes. So, in the tradition of Nehemiah, he set out to exhort his small Christian community to build the walls of their school, one family at a time. However, he first needed some land. He also needed some money.

Dan's plan was simple and challenging. He would design and build a school that was self-contained and within one building. The building would house up to 750 students. It could be built for less money and expanded as the needs occurred. It would include a gym, stage, and cafeteria in the middle. Classrooms were to ring the perimeter of the center with extra classes upstairs. It was designed around a unique philosophy of ministry.

Dan urged his families (a couple of dozen) to begin to pray and seek the Lord on how He might have them participate. In short order, he had a core of volunteers. Plumbers, electricians, and carpenters all threw their hats into the ring. When he was ready to order supplies he found many people, Christians and non-Christians, willing to simply donate the goods to the school. Dan found that as he clearly communicated God's vision for the school, people caught the vision and wanted to help.

Dan's group only raised $4,000 to start the project. Being short on cash and still without land, Dan put an offer on a coveted plot of ground. The owner told Dan he had one other offer that was considerably higher than Dan's group could afford. Only a zoning issue, a formality really, stood in the way of the sale being transacted. Dan asked the man to contact the school should the current deal fall through.

Time passed and Dan noticed the land was not being developed. He called to check on the progress of the deal. The owner was beside himself with anger towards the city, which had betrayed him by rezoning the property. It killed his deal. He was so upset that he offered to sell Dan the land for the amount at which it was purchased over ten years ago. By Dan's calculations, it was a saving of well over $350,000.

In April word got out that the new Christian school would be opening its doors. That left only four months to build a 60,000 square-foot building. Dan and the school board seized on the opportunity to further challenge their friends and families. A deluge of free gifts-in-kind and labor poured into the project. Dan kept detailed records of all God was doing.

In September the school opened its doors. Start to finish, from the dream to the completion, had been less than one year! Dan began to recognize the importance of sharing with others the story of God's blessing. Today Dan Cook and Associates (DCA) is a very successful company helping dozens of Christian schools begin their building process God's way, using Nehemiah as the biblical model.

Prayer changes things. Remember my pastor friend and his wife? Well, true to their word, they spent a fair bit of time stirring things up. I was dragged through the mud a little. Things got ugly, very ugly for the next few months. In fact, I had never felt so isolated and alone. My only solace was Jesus.

Jesus was not my first choice. I preferred to answer back. I wanted to defend myself, to clear my name. I had proof; I was right! I was standing for godliness! Darn it, I was God's man in the midst of severe persecution.

My only solace was Jesus. Sometimes in the ministry we pray and God says to just let it be. Don't pursue your rights. Don't brag on your accomplishments. Don't seek damages, apologies, or public reinstatement. Just let it be. Like Jacob, I wrestled with God over how unfair it all was. I had a friend in the ministry tell me that problems from the past are like cat poop. Don't jiggle it, don't touch it, for if you do the stink will be most unfortunate. When dealing with past issues, like cat poop, it is sometimes better to just let it be.

A long time passed before I could just let it be. Interestingly, though, once I realized the school, the ministry, and my life all belonged to God, it didn't matter who was right. I no longer cared what people thought of me. I was not interested in revisiting the situation with people "wanting to help." I had given up my rights to pursue my responsibility of serving Jesus. As soon as I came to this realization, I was free to love this family who had hurt me so badly.

Actually, their venom and bitterness toward me had consumed *their* lives. Though I had been praying for them throughout the ordeal, I had never done so with a whole heart. That is, until God's peace had relieved me of my own fermenting anger and bitterness. I realized I was becoming the very feeling that obsessed me each day. In praying for the family, I asked God to lovingly show them how they could understand what had happened and why it had happened.

One day a member of their church came up after a service and told them God directed them to "get their house in order." He also gave them the Scripture, "Fathers correct your children for in so doing, you will have peace." (Proverbs 29:17) Then the church member gave them the following note, which, according to the family, broke them open unto the Lord.

Parent, your child is speaking. "Mom, Dad, don't forget the purpose of your discipline is for me to learn from you. Don't be afraid to be firm with me; I prefer it. It lets me know where I stand. Don't only use force with me; that teaches me that power is all that counts. I will respond more readily by being led and by being taught.

Please don't be inconsistent; that confuses me and will make me try harder to get away with everything I can. Don't make me feel smaller than I am. That may cause me to make up for it by behaving like a big shot.

Mom, Dad, don't do things for me that I can do myself. It makes me feel like a baby. Don't correct me in front of other people; I prefer to talk quietly in private. Don't ever think it is beneath your dignity to apologize to me. An honest apology makes me feel surprisingly warm toward you. Don't try to preach to me. You'd be surprised how well I already know what's right and what's wrong. Don't tax my honesty too much. I'm easily frightened into telling lies. Don't make promises unless you are able or mean to keep them. That destroys my confidence in you.

Please don't call my mistakes sins. I have to learn to make mistakes without feeling that I am no good. Please don't nag. If you do, I shall have to protect myself by appearing deaf.

Don't always expect explanations for my misbehavior. Sometimes I don't really know why I did it. Don't forget that I can't thrive without lots of understanding and lots of encouragement. I will do almost anything for your approval.

One thing more, Mom, Dad. I learn a lot more from you as a model than as a critic or activist."

God is faithful. The passion to begin a new or rebuilding work in Christian schools is infectious. Obey God's call with fervor and hopefulness. God's protection of our lives will supercede personality or position. His protection is always timely and secure. God's provision will include needs which are physical as well as spiritual and emotional. In the end the Christian educator's life should lead to one singular accusation. The Christian ministry, too, must be about only one thing: Just Jesus.

CHAPTER
three

Foundational Excellence

Where there is no counsel, the people fall; But in the multitude of counselors there is safety.

                                            Proverbs 11:14

MODELS OF BOARD GOVERNANCE

People come first. The people leading a Christian school dictate the philosophy, vision, and implementation within the Christian school. The excellent Christian school has a clearly defined form of government. The government structure of every Christian school fits into one of four models of biblical governance: Congregational, Episcopal, Presbyterian and Mosaic.

    The Congregational form of church / school government is a uniquely American invention and appeals to our sense of democracy. Basically, the congregation or parent group as a whole makes all decisions by voting on matters of importance and appointing committees from its ranks to run the daily operation of the school. Most Congregational, Baptist, Pentecostal, Brethren, and non-denominational church schools are organized in this fashion. The congregation votes on hiring the school leader, votes on how to spend the money, and on anything else of importance. Although democratic people like the idea, congregational forms of school government often wind up causing the school leader to be directed by the sheep he is supposed to lead, and at worst this situation reduces the pastor to a hireling.

The Episcopal form of church / school government, used by Episcopalian, Anglican, Catholic, Orthodox, and Methodist church / schools (to name a few), is controlled by a church hierarchy, which may have differing names. Basically, there is a bishop, or someone of similar stature if called by a different name, who oversees the church / school, appoints pastors / administrators, sets policies, and guides the vision of the local congregations. Unfortunately, this style of government, which grew out of the European monarchies, leaves little freedom for the pastor / administrator or people to follow the leading of the Spirit.

The Presbyterian form of church / school government, which is typical in Presbyterian and Reformed churches, puts the decisions of church / school policy in the hands of a select group of elders (the "presbytery") who are appointed in various different ways, depending on the church / school organization. These elders are over the pastor / administrator, who in turn is over the congregation. Like the congregational model, the problem here is that this system puts the God-appointed leader under some of those he is supposed to lead.

The Mosaic model of governance takes both Moses and Jesus as the biblical reference. In this form of governance, the head of the school is responsible to hear from God. This person is responsible to feed and love the people faithfully. Elders or board members are appointed to help the leader care for the spiritual and philosophical needs of the people and school. The board is established for one purpose only, which is to serve.

In the Mosaic model, the head of the school may be a pastor, superintendent, or headmaster. The Mosaic model is bereft of tanglesome committees and subcommittees. This form of government is very streamlined, not a complex bureaucracy. The school leader guides the school as the Holy Spirit leads him. Faith in God and trust that He has called and anointed the leader is essential in the Mosaic model.

In the Mosaic model, church or school organization is de-emphasized. The positive side of this style of governance is a streamlined, highly efficient and expedient organization. The downside is the possibility of one man leading the ministry astray. Likewise, a cult of personality may emerge if Jesus is not front and center in all things. Like Moses and Jesus, this style is high on delegation and discipleship.

In each of these models of governance, Christian school leaders must be willing to follow James in his definition of wisdom. "But the wisdom that is from above is first pure, then peaceable, gentle, willing to yield, full of mercy and good fruits, without partiality and without hypocrisy. Now the fruit of righteousness is sown in peace by those who make peace" (James 3: 17–18). Leaders lead by example. The Christian leader's example must always point to Jesus.

Christian school leaders must be fanatical about their desire to forgo their own agendas. Christian school leaders provide a powerful witness to children and families as well as faculty, staff, and the community at large. That witness can be holy or horrific. Christian school leaders must be willing to sacrifice. Sacrifice is not reflected in being right instead of yielding, being proud instead of humble, being quick to judge instead of being merciful, and talking the talk without walking the walk.

The following story illustrates the heart of true sacrifice. I received this from Bob Johnson via the internet.

Many years ago, when I worked as a volunteer at Stanford Hospital, I got to know a little girl named Liz who was suffering from a rare and serious disease. Her only chance of recovery appeared to be a blood transfusion from her five-year-old brother, who had miraculously survived the same disease and had developed the antibodies, needed to combat the illness. The doctor explained the situation to her little brother, and asked the boy if he would be willing to give his blood to his sister. I saw him hesitate for only a moment before taking a deep breath and saying, "Yes I'll do it if it will save Liz." As the transfusion progressed, he lay in bed next to his sister and smiled, as we all did, seeing the color return to her cheeks. Then his face grew pale and his smile faded. He looked up at the doctor and asked with a trembling voice, "Will I start to die right away?" Being young, the boy had misunderstood the doctor. He thought he was going to have to give his sister all of his blood.

Again, sacrifice foregoes self.

Board Purpose

The excellent Christian school will develop some type of governing body be it Congregational, Episcopal, Presbytery or Mosaic. This group will be wholly dedicated to serving one another as well as the school. When, not if, but *when* conflict arises, those serving the Christian school must surrender their perceived rights and proposed needs. The laying aside of individual agendas in humble sacrifice is the very least a biblically focused governing body can do.

Prayer is foundational to the success of any board. Prayer to God Almighty is the great arbitrator. If after prayer there is still no resolution on an issue, then the board must wait. Waiting on the Lord is essential to growing in the Lord. Loving one another should be the outward fruit of the board. Jesus said that people would know we are Christians because of our love for one another.

The board's highest priority is to pray for, hire, and support the chief administrator. The board's second priority is to get out of the way and let the administrator administrate. It is a simple relationship. In general, if the administrator is not called of God, the administrator should leave once they realize this. If not, the board should pray and ask the administrator to leave as the Lord leads. Prayerful, loving confrontation is necessary for a healthy Christian school to excel.

In general, boards provide protection and wisdom to the administration. Healthy boards help establish philosophies of ministry and operation. One example would be the school's mission statement. They may also help design general policy directions for the school. For instance, "The school will pursue Christian texts or accreditation to be successfully completed within the next five years."

Christian school boards must never, ever interfere with the day-to-day operations of the Christian school. All questions, comments, and concerns should be taken to the administrator one-on-one, outside the school's normal daily operating schedule. Too often Christian schools become the scandal *du jour* in their communities because of loose lips or other indiscretions. The name of Jesus Christ must, in all things, supercede the wisdom of man. The witness of the school is the witness of its leadership.

One time, a lay person said of a preacher, "I'm sorry Pastor. I can't hear your message on Sunday; your witness is speaking louder than your teaching." How awful if the

Christian school meets budgets, graduates students, has a nice facility but has a sorry witness. The witness of the leadership of the school is the testimony of the school. Understand this; it is foundational to true excellence. The following story illustrates this in part.

Francis of Assisi once invited an apprentice to go with him to a nearby village to preach. The young monk quickly agreed, seizing an opportunity to hear his teacher speak. When they arrived in the village, St. Francis began to visit the people.

First he stopped in on the butcher. Next, a visit with the cobbler. Then a short walk to the home of a woman who'd recently buried her husband. After that, a stop at the school to chat with the teacher. This continued throughout the morning. After some time, Francis told his disciple that it was time to return to the abbey.

The student didn't understand. "But we came to preach," he reminded. "We haven't preached a sermon."

"Haven't we?" questioned the elder. "People have watched us, listened to us, responded to us. Every word we have spoken, every deed we have done has been a sermon. We have preached all morning." Pausing, Francis concluded, "my dear child, preach without ceasing. If you must, use words."

The heart to serve God must flow through all the areas of the excellent Christian school. The Christian school is unique in that God dwells within its operations. The board must be vigilant to pray for any part of the school that is grieving the Holy Spirit. One sure way to tell if a school is grieving the Spirit of God is to check the Word of God. God will not contradict the Bible.

Administrative and Board Relations

The following examples are all true. They may be difficult to read but are necessary to report. They are included because oftentimes we would rather bury our heads than seek solutions. Though traumatic, there are blessings in each story, as well. Here are stories from three types of board models. Perhaps you have experienced one or more yourself.

The first is the Congregational model. In one year, at two Christian schools twenty minutes apart, the congregational model of governance changed the Christian educational direction for an entire region. In one instance, a headmaster with an EdD in administration was literally voted out of his position by a vote of 52 percent to 48 percent. In another instance a veteran headmaster with his doctorate was pressured out of his position by the threat of a vote from a vocal critic.

The first situation was traumatic in that the headmaster had been at the helm for over six years. He had instituted many essential and meaningful programs. These innovations included technology, language, growing the school through the twelfth grade, seeing over 300 percent growth and more. The problem regarded the way he had expelled the son of a deacon in the church. Not only that, but during the expulsion the pastor had discovered the parent / deacon was not faithful in some crucial duties.

The expulsion of the child had precipitated the dismissal of the parent / deacon from leadership. That is, until a new pastor was voted in three years later. That parent / deacon found a way back into leadership under the new pastor. He eventually built enough of a case and caused so much turmoil against the headmaster that the congregation was forced into a vote of confidence in the headmaster. The vote was 52 percent against and 48 percent for the headmaster. The renegade parent had been used to provoke change. That school two years later is still in a state of deep crisis. The administrator was offered a position at a school 600 miles away.

The second instance saw an administrator with over eight years experience so pressured by a core constituency in the church that he simply preferred to resign and move on. The tragedy here was that the issues were incidental to personality conflicts. In numerous instances the administrator agreed with the groups' recommendations and implemented them successfully. The core issue dealt with a desire to destroy the character and authority of the administrator.

Time after time the administrator was forced to spend time and energy defending himself rather than promoting the school. Rumors fueled by angry, misinformed and, in some instances, mean-spirited people caused great confusion and concern within the school community. The threat of a congregational vote on his continued ministry was too much to bear. Rather than cause a great schism, he choose to resign and move on. God blessed him by allowing him to return to his home area to administer a new Christian school. Romans 8:28 is still in operation.

In the congregational model, by far the greatest strength is the idea of "massive action." The congregational form of governance is superb when the body is unified, especially on a specific task such as a "barn raising." One example of this is a Mennonite church in our area that prayed, listened to God, obeyed, and built a brand new sanctuary and 85,000 square foot school house for less than a million dollars in about seven months. They also did it with no debt.

In the second example, the Presbyterian model of governance, another friend of mine experienced the strong wisdom of a group of people dedicated to not rushing to judgment on many difficult and complicated issues. In this system, because it relies on the continual counsel of the entire board, it took a long time to come to decisions on some critical personal issues. During these times of waiting, God had ample time to resolve virtually all of these issues, without the board needing to get fully involved. Longer decisions can make people feel as though the system has been exhausted or they have been forgotten.

My friend's first year as headmaster was a doozy! He came into a situation knowing that God had called him and his family. He figured that would suffice. Surprise, surprise! It is important to not only answer the call, but also to ask questions of the constituency, students, parents, teachers, board and community. He didn't, but he should have.

In the first week on the job, a teacher he had just met showed complete defiance toward him by announcing she would sit in on a meeting he was having "whether he liked it or not." In very short order things went downhill. Approximately 25 percent of the staff, mostly veteran teachers, had become very angry, very vocal, and very bitter upon his introduction as headmaster. He later learned that the school had been run by a board with no administrative head for two years. Prior to that, the headmaster left because of burnout. The teachers had been used to running the show.

In one instance he was forced to confront the most vocal and vitriolic faculty member on the issue of gossip / slander. She had represented to a board member that he was requiring the faculty to be involved in policies and doctrine that was not only against the mission of the school, but unscriptural and morally offensive to her. He attempted to discuss the issue with her one-on-one, as per the dictates of Matthew 18. She demanded that he not speak to her again on the issue. Since the teacher had spoken to a board member, my friend requested that board member and the chairman of the board be present for the next attempt at a meeting.

Fortunately, in the Presbyterian style of governance, the board takes much of the responsibility for final arbitration in matters of grievance. Since the problems in the school faculty were surfacing in one form or another all year, the board was able to use time as a factor in settling truth from error, fact from fiction. In my friend's case, God had provided the perfect witness in his meeting with the furious teacher.

The chairman and administrator sat through hours and hours of this woman screaming, threatening, essentially vomiting up all over on a wide variety of subjects, and finally quitting. She later blamed them for firing her. That one stirred the hornets nest a little. It took about seven months for most people to see the real conflict was not about this hideous new headmaster. It was about vision, philosophy, and style. Those called to the new work stayed. Those not called left. Unfortunately, many left bitter and hurt rather than humble and blessed.

The Presbyterian style of governance allowed things to play out to the point that not one of the people who left the school was asked to leave by the administration. God had called people in and out of the school in His timing for His purpose. It was a shame that so many good Christians had allowed the school to become their own private club. It happens all the time in Christian schools. Those called to start the work end up owning the work because God moved in an original way once upon a time in their school experience. Beware of God's work growing from a movement to a monument to a memorial to a mausoleum. Christians tend to grieve the Spirit of God and then ask why has He not moved recently like He "used to."

Examples of grieving the Holy Spirit include subtle

racism, favoritism (especially to church leaders), and unresolved hard feelings in leadership, that include bitterness, envy, slander, and gossip. Pride, trying to build a cause against the school, and common sin such as adultery or theft clearly grieve God's Spirit. There are many other types of sin, as well. Suffice it to say that the top two sins in ministry are failure to take responsibility for one's own actions and jumping on someone else's "little red band wagon."

The third is a Mosaic style. The pastor was God's anointed. He, in turn, gave enormous freedom to those in the ministry under his authority. It seemed exciting to serve such a man of faith. In this model, when the Holy Spirit was grieved, the fruit always found its pungent way back to the pastor. He would then check in with the administrator, offer wisdom, and the administrator could make a rather quick decision. Quick decisions can make people feel heard or put off. Quick decisions made in a vacuum allow the people closest to the decisionmaker to feel honored and heard. However, those not near the inner circle can feel put off and outside the leadership team. Sometimes the decisions have larger ramifications.

In one example, the administrator was called into the pastor's office in the fall of his third year as principal. The seventh through twelfth-grade school had expanded from sixty students to over 250 in two short years. Along with that wonderful growth had come different types of behavioral challenges. Among the most prevalent were smoking cigarettes, drinking alcohol, and smoking pot. A number of students had been caught at a recent school sponsored event. One of those students was the child of a very good friend of the pastor, an assistant pastor's child.

Immediately upon entering the office, the administrator sensed this was more than a fact-finding mission. The pastor and the assistant pastor were both in the meeting. The administrator was asked why they were having so many problems. They asked why they were letting in so many kids of bad influence (obviously referring to all but the assistant pastor's son). The principal thought, "You are kidding, right?"

In very short order he explained that the children allowed into the school were the very children of parents to which the church ministers on Sundays. In no uncertain terms, he offered that not only should they continue to admit students that meet the school's standards, but also to love them with a biblical love when, not if, they fail. Most teenage children will fall into temptation. The Bible is clear on this matter. The prodigal son is one example.

The Bible warns us that "Sin is pleasurable for a season" (Hebrews 11:25). Our responsibility as Christians is to "train up a child up in the way he should go, and when he is old he will not depart from it" (Proverbs 22:6). Very quickly the pastor moved from shutting the school down because of the sinful witness, to supporting the school in every way possible. The assistant pastor was heartsick that the ruling to suspend the children was not overturned. He felt both heard and put off. He felt heard in that the issue was diagnosed, dealt with and a solution arrived at. He felt put off in that his sense at that time of the correct response to things was ignored.

In time, the assistant pastor became one of the strongest supporters of the school. God used the circumstance in his life to prepare him and his family for an expansion of his ministry. The pastor's faithfulness to God's vision, and his desire to search out all the facts led to not only preserving the integrity of the school ministry, but also growing others in the direction of God's new call on their lives. The Mosaic model is particularly effective when it comes to quick and decisive action. It is also a strong discipleship model.

ADMINISTRATIVE AND BOARD ACCOUNTABILITY

An administrator friend of mine shared the following story with me.

> *My wife and I spent the first year of our new call visiting a number of local churches. Our intent was to find a church where we could fellowship and grow in the Lord. In the small town where we moved, we instead found unbearable expectations.*
>
> *I was asked to serve as both a deacon and elder in one church. Another pastor informed me that God told him I was to come alongside and serve the Lord with him in leadership in his church. In more than a few churches, my wife and I were expected to rotate into the childcare and nursery ministries, help feed in the food and rainment ministry, and come early and stay late helping to set up chairs or tear them down. It was the first time we ever dreaded going to church.*

Leaders of Christian schools are in constant danger of being overused in the ministry. The natural expectation is, if you are in the ministry during the week, then you must be good at it. It is presumed that your spiritual gifts will easily transfer. This is all well and good if you are called to help in your local church. Peer pressure or even a need is not enough reason to step in and help. God must call each person into his or her respective ministries.

A simple rule of thumb in these situations is if you are performing ministry where God has not called you, look out! Two things are liable to happen; neither is good. First, you may be blocking the growth in another person whom the Lord desires to challenge. Second, you will be expending valuable time and resources to do something that God may not necessarily have for you. Consider, for example, Moses defending the Israelite being beaten by the Egyptian guard. Moses murdered the guard, clearly not God's desire. Moses then spent much time and energy running from, and trying to live down, a situation in ministry in which he had no business being involved.

In short, Christian school leadership must find a church in which to worship God. Anything short of the unfettered ability to personally enter into intimate worship with God is useless and unprofitable. Service to God in one's church is fine. It must not be presumed or obligatory. The health of the school depends on a prospering relationship between the school leadership and the Lord. Church is a big part of this. Do not be pressured into filling other peoples' expectations. Go find a place you can worship God.

EVALUATION

In the area of yearly evaluations it is important that the school board follow the same systems the school leadership and faculty follow. The reason for this is that it helps build unity and understanding and promotes common accountability. One example of this is a yearly "Dreams and Goals" session. In January of every year, every faculty, staff, administrator, and board member is required to complete a packet, which includes the following instructions:

1. List three personal and three professional goals you wish to accomplish in the next year.

2. Explain how you have improved in your ministry this year and how you plan on continuing to improve.

3. Has God called you back to the ministry next year?

4. A personal inventory sheet, which asks questions such as the name of member's church and Bible study,

dedication to devotional time, tools used daily, and more.

In addition, each person is required to meet with the school principal and the headmaster for a brief forty-five minute discussion, time of prayer, and fellowship. It is this follow-up meeting that is crucial to the success of the vision and the unity of the school for the upcoming school year. The board president meets with the headmaster and each board member. The board president and the headmaster hold one another accountable.

During the Dreams and Goals meeting, faculty and staff not being invited back next year are alerted to that fact. The reasons should be specific and well documented over time. In such cases it is always better to break the news at the outset of the meeting, directly after prayer. It is important to be clear and compassionate, but firm. Eye contact is crucial. The school leadership must speak the truth in love. Remember, love is also being honest enough to allow someone to find what God has next for him or her.

BIBLICAL AUTHORITY

A final note on the board, headmaster, and leadership of the Christian school: It is impossible and terribly unwise for anyone in leadership to assume the mantle of "expert." Trying to accomplish the things of the Lord in a humanly manner will result in unfortunate calamity. This may be the most important warning in this chapter. It is subtle, insidious, and it was the very sin of Lucifer. He declared, "I will be like the Most High" (Is. 14:14). It would be wisdom in its simplest form to often recall from memory the Scripture,

"Not by might nor by power, but by My Spirit," says the Lord.

Zechariah 4:6

Biblical authority is given directly from God to man. Man is given a certain freedom in exercising God's delegated authority. This freedom is reflected in the four distinct governing styles mentioned here. In any event, it is imperative for everyone involved in the Christian school to be taught, to understand and to obey the biblical authority in the Christian school. This responsibility begins with the person or group charged with leading the school. Watchman Nee said it best: "If you want to be in authority you must be under authority."

Biblical authority can be broken down in a simplified manner as follows:

1. Authority is from God. (Matthew 28:18)
2. God delegates authority to man. (1 Timothy 2:1–2)
3. To be in authority you must first be under authority. (Romans 13:1–14)
4. God's law is perfect. It involves cause and effect. (Psalms 19)
    a. Practical law—Rules that help things run better.
    b. Principle law—Precepts based upon biblical truth, specific law. (1 Sam 16:23)
    c. Precept law—Clear commandments of God.
5. Biblical Appeal. (Esther Chapters 2–4)
    a. Pray.
    b. Seek God's will.
    c. Have courage and remove pride.
    d. Speak the truth in integrity.
    e. Earnestly trust God.
    f. Accept the decision ("If I perish, I perish.")
6. Biblical Relationships: How to handle interpersonal problems.

a. Listen. (James 1:19–20)
b. Search out facts. (Proverbs 18:13)
c. Examine yourself first. (Matthew 7:1–15)
d. Go first to the person. (Matthew 18:15)
e. Be honest. (Ephesians 4:25)
f. Be correct. (Ephesians 4:3)
g. No 100 percent statements. (Colossians 4:6)
h. Go with a right spirit. (Ephesians 4:29)
i. Do not attack the person. (Ephesians 4:29)
j. Act, don't react. (Ephesians 4:31–33)
k. Love one another. (Romans 12)

Note: The #1 problem in ministry is the failure of people to handle problems correctly. The #2 problem in ministry is people picking up others' offenses. Honor your word. Trust God. Do not jump on another's "little red bandwagon."[2]

In our ministry we have three simple rules for any meeting, discussion, or other school-wide area of potential impact. The three rules are:

1. Everything but the school vision is on the table, there are no "sacred cows."
2. Attack issues, not people.
3. Feel free to offer concerns and suggestions, but please provide at least one potential solution.

The administration and board must be prepared to risk reputation and position in order to do the right thing. The administration and board must, as a matter of conscience, do the right thing because it is right to do the right thing. In some cases the administration and board may have to risk friendships, family outrage, or societal pressures in the pursuit of God's will and to do what is right in a matter. Integrity and service are inseparable for the excellent

Christian school administration and board. The following story from my friend Bob Johnson illustrates this very pivotal point.

> *One night at 11:30 p.m., an older African-American woman was standing on the side of an Alabama highway, trying to endure a lashing rainstorm. Her car had broken down, and she desperately needed a ride. Soaking wet, she decided to flag down a car.*
>
> *A young white man stopped to help her—generally unheard of in those conflict-filled 1960s. The man took her to safety, helped her get assistance, and put her into a taxicab. She seemed to be in a big hurry! She wrote down his address, thanked him, and drove away.*
>
> *Seven days went by and a knock came on the man's door. To his surprise, a giant console TV was delivered to his home. A special note was attached. It read:*
>
>> Thank you so much for assisting me on the highway the other night. The rain drenched not only my clothes but also my spirits. Then you came along.
>>
>> Because of you, I was able to make it to my dying husband's bedside just before he passed away. God bless you for helping me and unselfishly serving others.
>>
>> Sincerely,
>> Mrs. Nat King Cole

In the final analysis, the board's primary focus should be threefold. First, keep Jesus at the center of all the school does. Second, fan the fire of vision throughout the school community. Do this by looking to the future, living in the future, and developing the future for the school. Third, seek creative ways to implement the school vision in support of the chief administrator. Never settle for the obvious when God may have so much more for the ministry if the board will just wait and expect the simple, yet unexpected, blessings of God. Sometimes the board and administration will need take the road less traveled.

I came upon three men one day and asked the following question:

"If the earth was going to be covered with twenty feet of water in three days what would you do?" The first man said, "I would live my life to the fullest doing everything I always wanted." The second man said, "I would pay all my debts and make friends with all my enemies." The third man thought for a moment and replied, "I'd learn to live under water."

Author Unknown

Remember what is considered logical and innovative today will be ineffective and meaningless tomorrow. Leaders need to pray for God's fresh wisdom daily. Do not settle for the "old manna" of times past. Proverbs 3:5–6 says it best: "Trust in the Lord with all your heart, and lean not on your own understanding; In all your ways acknowledge Him and He will direct your paths."

Simple wisdom is usually the best wisdom. God selects men to lead His sheep. Leadership has its own set of fundamentals critical to the pursuit of excellence in the Christian school. Christian schools must "get it right" the first time in selecting the leadership structure and leaders that best meet the needs of the ministry and community. Failure to build the proper leadership foundation will be like building a house of cards on a hill of sand.

CHAPTER
four

Leadership and Love

But the greatest of these is love.

1 Corinthians 13:13

STYLE

I was eighteen years old and had just been promoted from night closer to night shift manager at a national fast food franchise. I was suddenly responsible for approximately twenty people. The same people I had been working alongside were now under my authority. In a sense, I was now their boss, at least from 4:00 p.m. till 1:00 a.m. I felt strange, very strange.

Many questions ran through my mind that first night following my promotion. These same questions would resurface whenever I was offered a new leadership position. The questions include, What am I supposed to accomplish here? Do I have a vision or direction for this organization? Assuming I do know where to go next, how do I get others to go with me? What if I ask someone to do something and they refuse, or worse, ignore me?

That first night I was finishing a book on Israeli military history. In reading this book, I was humbled, saddened, and amazed at how often Israeli officers are killed in action during any given conflict. The conclusion drawn by the author clearly suggested that this was the defining, intangible strength that separated the Israeli fighter from soldiers in any other standing army. The Israeli armed forces were consistently led in combat by their highest ranking officers.

This simple and heroic revelation deeply impacted my view of leadership, and I believe that it will continue to influence me for the rest of my life. In studying the lives of King David, Nehemiah, Jesus, Paul, and others, it became increasingly clear to me that the best leaders lead with their lives. That is to say, they lead by being in front, not in the rear. There is a pithy quote some prominent business leaders post on their desks. It reads: "Lead, follow, or get out of the way." Though brusque, the clarity is compelling.

People follow people who lead honestly. Great leaders lead with a passion born of personal commitment. I thought I would have a panic attack on my first night as manager; my throat felt like a Brillo pad. My heart raced like a model airplane with a wing chopped off. The sweat from my arms made me look like a very bad comic in a Gong Show gig. I was a mess.

The only thing I could think of was, as time passed and specific jobs went untouched, "I need to lead by showing them first." So, instead of asking a crewmember to sweep, I grabbed the broom. I first assigned breaks to everyone else, then I took mine. Instead of staying in the office at closing time, I helped clean fryers, shake machines, and bathrooms.

The crew was so amazed. That night the crew leader took a broom from my hand and said he would take care of that for me from now on. That first night I learned the value of leading by example. Three years later, that same crew would win a regional award for Best Trained Crew.

VISION

The speed of the leader is the speed of the team. I've heard this dozens of times at various business functions throughout the years. Though simplistic it is true. Leaders that are out of sight are also out of mind. People don't want to follow someone they can't see. For a leader, visibility is critical. Strong leaders are physically visible. They physically touch people. The superior leader stops, looks into people's eyes, shakes hands, and listens. The example is Jesus. He allowed people to touch Him.

"And suddenly, a woman who had a flow of blood for twelve years came from behind and touched the hem of His garment. For she said to herself, 'If only I may touch His garment, I shall be made well.' But Jesus turned around, and when He saw her He said, 'Be of good cheer, daughter; your faith has made you well.' And the woman was made well from that hour" (Matthew 9:20–22).

He touched people. "When Jesus departed from there, two blind men followed Him, crying out and saying, 'Son of David, have mercy on us!' And when He had come into that house, the blind men came to Him. And Jesus said to them, 'Do you believe that I am able to do this?' They said to Him, 'Yes, Lord.' Then He touched their eyes, saying, 'According to your faith let it be to you.' And their eyes were opened" (Matthew 9: 27–30).

Vision and accessibility go hand in hand. Leaders must have vision and must lead where the people can see them. That means not too far out front where people lose sight of you and the vision. Likewise, not so close that the people overtake the vision and it becomes lost in competing viewpoints and opinions.

Vision is a catalyst for the mind. Leadership drives

the dream. Administration orders the vision. Teamwork determines the level of commitment and degree of excellence in an organization. People follow people who follow the vision.

The more often the vision is stated, the better chance the school family will understand and respond to the leadership. A vision is a goal; leadership is the power source for the goal; and people are the means the Lord uses to achieve the goal. Vision clarifies by liberating peoples' thinking toward one common focus. Vision helps eliminate unnecessary energy and time spent toward accomplishing a goal. Leaders must help people reach the vision by encouraging people to grow beyond their comfort zones.

One year we scheduled a faculty and staff retreat. Not a big deal, really, except it was six hours away and was a two-day, two-night retreat. It was scheduled a year in advance and was explained often throughout the school year. Still, two weeks before orientation began a number of faculty and staff began to panic.

You can probably imagine. Can't you? The concerns poured in. "How could we require people to leave their families?" And, "Didn't God say our families were more important than our vocations even if we were in the ministry?" By the time we were a day away from departing, people were telling us they "would not go."

I received a phone call from a very influential school member the week prior to leaving. He said, "Chapin, these people are being stretched well beyond what is reasonable and you are causing division where I believe your intent is to bring unity. I am telling you in the strongest possible terms to cancel the trip this year and reevaluate the purpose for coming years. I would hate to see all we have worked for flushed down the drain."

I had a choice. You do too when these challenges come

your way. "Did I miss God on this?" "Should I cancel for the greater good of those most uncomfortable with my decision?" "What are the consequences if we do move forward?"

My first reaction (after being stunned and scared silly) was to pray with the caller. Then I sought to roust up our trusty ministry prayer support team. Next I tried to re-surrender the whole affair to the Lord. This was difficult because I could only focus on failure. I failed if I cancelled and admitted I had "missed the Lord." I also failed if we went and the division did occur. The only hope was in the Lord.

After much prayer and support through prayer, I believed we were supposed to stay the course. The vision God had given me was of Jesus and the disciples getting away to the mountains. I had put my trust in the Scripture, "And we know that all things work together for good to those who love God, to those who are the called according to His purpose" (Romans 8:28). I would like to say I boldly went forward but, in reality, I closed my eyes and pointed ahead with the words, "We are going up the hill."

Upon my arrival the camp director told me no one had shown up yet. It was an hour past arrival time and I had left after everyone else. The director asked me, "How many do you expect?" We had eighty plus on staff, but I had hoped originally for fifty-five or sixty to come. I told the director that at this point, I would welcome two dozen.

I went into the woods to meditate on my untimely demise. Returning in forty-five minutes I couldn't believe my eyes. There were dozens of cars, and dinner was being served to at least thirty-six people. I was encouraged. That night we filled the worship room. The director came by and whispered in my ear, "Chapin, we set up sixty chairs in here just like you prayed, the room is now full." He had the warmest smile I had seen in some time.

Like Elijah after the victory God provided in burning up the wood drenched in water, I remained fearful. How would Jezebel make her appearance? Remember how Jezebel, the wife of Ahab, had simply threatened Elijah and he ran for his life. This, after God had so remarkably provided and glorified Himself in Elijah's ministry. I too was worried where the next attack would come from.

Well, God continued to provide "big time." During a time of sharing on the last night, many people confessed their dread about coming to the retreat. Still more told how they had made plans to cancel at the last moment. One teacher hurt her foot the day prior to departure. She planned to tell her husband she wasn't going. But the instant she thought that, the Lord told her it would be fine to miss the trip, but she would "miss it." And it was on that trip that God met her in a special way.

In the end, everyone was blessed. Each person who went on the retreat drew closer to God and to one another. Fears and phobias were dispelled by the move of God's Spirit. Our school benefited in real and meaningful ways. On the way home I reflected upon the lessons God had taught me during the retreat.

First, pray and receive the vision for ministry from God alone. Second, verify it in Scripture. You will need the assurance only God's Word can provide when the rubber hits the road. Third, share the vision within a trusted core group prior to sharing with your general constituency. This will help round off some rough edges. Finally, be open to suggestions, corrections, and criticisms.

However, do not ever compromise the vision God has given you. The blessing of the Lord on the ministry and for the people He has entrusted us with requires you and me to move forward in spite of well meaning opposition or fierce attack. If

Leadership And Love 87

for some reason you have already made the error of caving to the pressure, be encouraged. The Bible has a fascinating side note to a story of lost vision in the midst of terrible internal attack and doubt.

Moses was leading the Israelites. God gave Moses specific instructions. "Then the Lord spoke to Moses, saying 'Take the rod; you and your brother Aaron gather the congregation together. Speak to the rock before their eyes, and it will yield its water; thus you shall bring water for them out of the rock, and give drink to the congregation and their animals'" (Numbers 20:7–8).

Notice the detail of God's request. Speak to the rock. Do it in front of the people. Do it with Aaron. Then, drink was provided for every person and his animals.

Notice what Moses did. He spoke to the people, not to the rock. "Hear now you rebels!" (Numbers 20:10). Moses reacted in anger toward the people, and the miracle's glory was lost when Moses demanded, "Must we bring water for you out of this rock?" (Numbers 20:10) Moses failed to do it with Aaron. Instead Moses, alone, "lifted his hand and struck the rock twice with his rod" (Numbers 20:11). However, God was faithful to fulfill His promise regardless of Moses' faithlessness, "and the congregation and their animals drank" (Numbers 20:11).

What happens next is as horrifying as it is bemusing. "Then the Lord spoke to Moses and Aaron, 'Because you did not believe Me, to hallow Me in the eyes of the children of Israel, therefore you shall not bring this assembly into the land which I have given them.'" (Numbers 20:12) Wow! How totally disappointing and devastating! That's it, Moses. One mistake and you miss the promise I have for you. It just seemed so harsh to me for so long. Until …

"Now after six days Jesus took Peter, James, and John

his brother, led them up on a high mountain by themselves, and He was transfigured before them. His face shone like the sun, and His clothes became as white as the light. And behold, Moses and Elijah appeared to them, talking with Him" (Matthew 17:1–3).

We know Moses died prior to the Israelites entering the Promised Land. We know God personally buried the body of Moses. We are sad and perplexed at the swiftness of God's judgment on Moses at the rock of Meribah. End of story, right?

Not exactly. You see God has a funny way of surprising us with His grace. The story of the water is deep. Perhaps deeper than this treatment, but here are a few insights as they pertain to vision and leadership:

Moses had a rod that probably had buds on it in the springtime; fruit, if you will. When he struck the rock he lost the fruit of his ministry. The rock he struck was symbolic of Jesus. Our reactions and responses to people always point them either toward or away from Jesus. The water represents the Holy Spirit. The fact the people and animals were given water in spite of Moses "misrepresenting" God should be a great comfort to us all.

Like you and me Moses was probably hurt, angry, and tired. His ministry "fell" because of the very thing that was his greatest strength. He loved the people too much. He needed to allow God to love and minister to the people in their rebellion. It was never Moses' responsibility to represent God's character in the ministry. God was quite capable of disciplining those folks in rebellion. God had not asked Moses to handle the rebellion on behalf of Moses.

So, Moses "blew it." What about hope for you and me? What if we blow it too? Aren't we living in the age of grace? Yes, and thankfully, Moses tasted God's grace too. Consider the Scripture, "And behold Moses and Elijah appeared to them, talking with Him" (Matthew 17:3). Answer the following questions, and you have a God-sized blessing on you hands: Where did Moses and Elijah appear? When did they appear? Why did they appear?

Well, Moses and Elijah appeared on the Mount of Transfiguration which, according to *The New Bible Dictionary* (p. 1212), was "probably Mt. Hermon, which rises to a height of 2,814 m. above sea level." Mt. Hermon is a "mountain in the Anti-Lebanon Range, and easily the highest in the neighborhood of Palestine." The answer to our first question is, God placed Moses and Elijah right in the Promised Land during the transfiguration. That's right, God snuck Moses into the Promised Land after all. Whew! That's great news!

The answer to when they appeared is simple. They appeared with Jesus to herald in the age of grace. Grace is what you and I breathe each day. Moses with Jesus was God's way of telling us believers that when, not if, but when we make a mistake, God will be there to surprise us with His grace and love.

Imagine how excited Moses must have been when he heard the Father say He would meet Jesus on a mountain in the place that God had promised him so long ago. How about you and me? Do we have promises from God that we lost long ago? Get ready, God may be preparing you for a transfiguration of your thinking. He may have a resurrection of a promise that just now you recall. Rejoice!

Finally, why did they appear on the Mount with Jesus? You and I need all the help we can get. Simply seeing Jesus with Moses brings to completion the transition between the Old and New Testaments. Grace supercedes the law. Moses in the flesh could not enter the Promised Land because he represented the law. God coming as a man in Jesus offers the ultimate sacrifice of grace on our behalf, wiping away the burden of the law.

I believe it is meant as an encouragement to us as well. Attack will come. Sometimes, like Moses, we will be so ensconced in the battle we will forget we are called to lead, not punish the people God has entrusted to us. Vision in Christian ministry of any kind requires a total sacrifice. Our lives must be dedicated to God. Our lives must be submitted in slavery to those we serve.

Attack will come, and when it does, it will eventually come against the vision. When that happens surrender it all back to Him. Let Him fight for you and me. "The Lord will fight for you, and you shall hold your peace" (Exodus 14:14). When you have "gone too far" do not despair, simply remember the story of Moses on the Mount of Transfiguration with Jesus. It will do your heart good.

Most attack we face in the ministry as it pertains to vision revolves around the sin of unbelief. Our unbelief or the unbelief of those around us constantly causes rabbit trails, derailments, or destruction within ministries each and every day. Our unbelief causes us to actually lose the blessings the Lord may have planned for us.

"When He had come to His own country, He taught them in their synagogue, so that they were astonished and said, 'Where did this Man get this wisdom and these mighty works? Is this not the carpenter's son? Is not His mother called Mary? And His brothers James, Joses, Simon, and Judas? And His sisters, are they not all with us? Where then did this Man get all these things?' So they were offended at Him. But Jesus said to them, 'A prophet is not without honor except in his own country and in his own house.' Now He did not do many mighty works there because of their unbelief" (Matthew 13:54–58).

In Hebrews, concerning Moses and the Israelites, it states, "So we see that they could not enter in because of unbelief" (Hebrews 3:19). Unbelief is the opposite of faith. It is "unfaith." When our vision is compromised by lack of faith, or unbelief, the ministry is bound to suffer. Remember, if you have "missed it" God can "redeem it." If you are struggling with attack and personal doubt, hold firm until God releases you through the Word, prayer, and godly counsel.

The Devil is the great counterfeit. God will confirm what is going on in your ministry. Ask Him, wait, and be faithful to what He says. Bring in as many core people to the decision making process as you can. Once you begin to raise up leadership around you, the vision of you ministry will expand in breadth and depth. Vision always promotes discipleship. Discipleship always promotes leadership. Leadership thrives or dies based on delegation.

Delegate

Delegate or die. Delegate and fly! Leaders who cannot delegate either burn out, rust out, or are thrown out. Leaders who can delegate see their ministry or business soar. I realized a long time ago that, as a leader, if I didn't cast and sustain the vision, delegate, and lead by example, then very little of consequence would take place. This is not more "leadership seminar drivel"; it is the truth.

Too many Christian schools are stagnating or are succumbing to disturbing infighting simply because the leadership has stopped leading and, instead, have become caretakers. The best leaders train people to replace themselves. Organizations mature into and develop the abilities of the leaders that lead them. Delegating is another method of raising people up in leadership.

Jesus was our finest example for expert leadership. Jesus

rested when His disciples thought He should be moving. Jesus constantly shared a vision of the future with everyone. Jesus not only delegated His earthly authority to disciples, but now through the Holy Spirit He gives us a supernatural authority to carry out His will in the here and now. Jesus gave us the finest example of leadership by example ever offered.

First, when He washed the disciples' feet he said, "If I then, your Lord and Teacher, have washed your feet, you also ought to wash one another's feet. For I have given you an example, that you should do as I have done to you" (John 13:14–15). Second, when He died on the cross for you and me, He gave us the ultimate gift of love. Leadership is ultimately about giving away everything, so that the only thing left is love.

One day I was making the rounds at our lower campus, which houses our preschool through fifth grades. It was my standard procedure as headmaster to visit each teacher, aide, and staff member at least once a week in their classroom or workplace environment. On this particular day I was in a bit of a hurry. I was less focused on "How may I serve you?" and more on going through the motions.

I noticed to my chagrin that the kindergarten aide was on her hands and knees picking up fragments of the ceiling tile. Her head and blouse were soaking wet. The children were in a tizzy. The teacher was at a loss. I was willing to help, although I had briefly considered walking the other way. I knew this was going to be the type of task that didn't get resolved in a few minutes.

I stepped into the room and offered to help. The teacher and aide said things would be fine. The roof leaked regularly, and now that the tiles were crumbling, the maintenance crew could see and repair the problem. I asked the aide to get cleaned up, and then spent some time personally cleaning up the floor, catching the leaking water, and helping to calm the excitement of the leak for the kindergarten class. Though taxed for time, I really didn't think much about it until a few weeks later, when I received a note from that classroom teacher. I believe it summarizes what God would say to those in leadership and administration. Here is what her note said:

Dear Chapin,

Isn't God good? In my study of 1 Corinthians 12 once again, I decided to check out the word "administration" in my expository. I was surprised to see it equated with the word minister, servant, and attendant. In Mark 10:43–44 is states, "Yet it shall not be so among you; but whoever desires to become great among you shall be your servant. And whoever of you desires to be first shall be slave of all."

I see a servant as the person who truly feels "How can I serve you?" and an attendant is one who goes one step further and says, "Let me do that for you." I couldn't help but remember the day you were there when our ceiling fell. You truly are an administrator according to the call of God. Thank you for your obedience.

Love ya,
Carol

Substance

Leadership is a call from God. Leadership requires sacrifice. Leadership will result in suffering. Leadership means the rights of an individual are given up and replaced by a definite sense of responsibility. Leadership requires a creative and flexible approach to living and ministering. Consider the tools Jesus used to move His ministry along.

Leighton Ford, in his book *Transforming Leadership*, notes:

> *Jesus gave up any right to independence; he was born in a borrowed manger, preached from a borrowed boat, entered Jerusalem on a borrowed donkey, ate the Last Supper in a borrowed upper room, died on a borrowed cross, and was buried in a borrowed tomb. In renouncing entitlement he exposed himself to temptation, sorrow, limitation and pain, and yet "although Jesus identified himself completely with us, he did not lose his own identity. He remained himself."*[3]

Leaders are readers. The type of person you wish to be five years from now is directly reflected by what you spend your time reading today. Leadership without love is manipulation. Leaders who promote an agenda without a relationship are called unemployed. Leaders need to devour literature in their field of call. Likewise, all that reading can make one dull to the heart of leadership, which is all about people. People don't make or break a leader, but the leader's approach to learning and people may.

WISDOM

Christian school leaders would never be accused of having it easy. In fact, Christians can be some of the meanest and most bitter people with which to deal. Often the problem is not the issue. The problem simply underscores a more deeply rooted disease that has been buried for years, sometimes since childhood. God uses Christian schools, and the conflict therein, to help refine those in leadership and to help heal those people coming into the school. Sometimes God has called the school educator or administrator to be faithful to share the love of Jesus in the midst of terrible personal attack. The biblical model for this is Proverbs 27:17, "As iron sharpens iron, So a man sharpens the countenance of his friend."

One time I experienced unrelenting gossip, slander, false accusations, and a devastating undermining of the authority and position in which God had placed me. At first I was amazed. In one instance, each time I spoke to the staff, a group of teachers gathered and handed me a Scripture that directly contradicted my message and tried to place an unnecessary blame or responsibility upon me. In time, as I waited and didn't react to them, the attacks became much more personal and pointed. Frankly, I thought that simply by the sheer volume of complaint I would be asked to leave the school. I waited on the Lord and watched intently.

During this time of horrendous attack, I learned a few valuable lessons. First, when someone comes to you and begins their complaint with an accusation, put-down, or other scurrilous comment, you can be assured the problem is with that person. It should be noted, however, that the Lord has brought them to your school to allow you to be the iron in the hand of the Lord to sharpen this person's countenance. Second, when a person brings a heartfelt complaint about a policy, program, or manner in which something was handled, pay very close attention. Here the Lord may be sharpening your countenance.

In the end, the Lord drew every single person out of the school in a manner which clearly communicated to the community and the people themselves that their time serving God in that particular ministry was through. We never had to fire a single person. The fruit upon their departure was unity, harmony, and love. The peace of the Lord guided us as we moved into a season of maturation and growth. However, it should be noted that Satan had desired to sift me like wheat during this trial. God's faithfulness overcame in spite of my weakness.

I distinctly recall times when I thought, "Let it be. It's not important enough to start another conflict over this matter." Issues of controversy were springing up out of thin air daily. On most days it was three and four issues about nothing, which then would flame into something that I simply could not ignore. In each instance my choices were: First, ignore the issue. Second, deal with the issue in a manner that placates the greatest number of folks, and try to move on as unhindered as possible to the next fire. Third, speak the truth in love.

The Bible tells us to speak the truth in love. The result is "the truth shall make you free" (John 8:32). Too often Christian school leaders bow to the pressures of the world. Those pressures range from not disciplining a child because they are family or friends of family, to ignoring a school policy in order to promote athletics, or worse. In some cases people will come to the school and swear that something is one way when it really is another way altogether. It is the administrator's job to cast the light of truth on circumstances that are muddled, manipulated, or simply misguided.

Truth hurts. Truth heals. Truth is a tool of wisdom. The Christian school leader must pray to God for the wisdom of Solomon. Too often in our society truth is considered relative. Situational ethics rule the educational landscape. Situational ethics says that it's fine to do what you want in any given situation so long as you either don't get caught or it doesn't directly hurt someone else. The entire abortion issue in our society is born out of this life philosophy.

Consider also the task of hiring and training the right faculty and staff. In many Christian schools the leadership relies on worldly techniques to select staff. God's thoughts are

Leadership And Love

not our thoughts. Nor are God's ways our ways. Remember God selected Mary and Joseph to raise His Son. God selected the shepherd boy David to be king. He chose a prostitute named Rahab to help save His people in Israel. Don't box God in.

Consider the following questions as they pertain to godly wisdom and leadership. How might you respond in the spur of the moment?

Q1: If you knew a woman who was pregnant, who already had eight kids, three of whom were deaf, two were blind, one mentally retarded, and she had syphilis: would you recommend that she have an abortion?

Q2: It is time to elect a world leader, and your vote when cast will be the deciding vote. Here are the facts about the three leading candidates:

A. Candidate A associates with crooked politicians, and consults with astrologists. He's had two mistresses. He also chain smokes and drinks ten martinis a day.

B. Candidate B was kicked out of office twice, sleeps until noon, used opium in college, and drinks a quart of whiskey every evening.

C. Candidate C is a decorated war hero. He's a vegetarian, doesn't smoke, drinks an occasional beer and hasn't had any extra-marital affairs.

Which of these candidates would be your choice?

Candidate A is Franklin D. Roosevelt

Candidate B is Winston Churchill

Candidate C is Adolf Hitler

And by the way, regarding the answer to the abortion question: if you suggested abortion, you just killed Beethoven!

Christian school leaders will be faced every day with

multiple decision making opportunities. Though few would bear the intense responsibility of those cited in the previous example, there will be those times of life-changing choices. The Christian school leader must be prayed up and sitting at the feet of the Lord daily to prevent being surprised or overwhelmed by the day-to-day ministry of Christian school education. The Bible tells us that wisdom is the principle thing, therefore get wisdom.

Heart

The greatest leaders give to serve not to receive. The greatest leaders give in service to the King of kings, not to promote their own agendas. The greatest leaders give of themselves in service to those under their authority, not for inducement or manipulation. God selects the greatest leaders. Man simply confirms what God has already done.

In Mark 10:43–44 we are told that "whoever desires to become great among you shall be your servant. And whoever of you desires to be first shall be slave of all." The world today exalts the individual far above any standards of right or wrong. Too often in the ministry the prevailing worldview takes center stage. True leadership dies daily to the insatiable appetite of the flesh. How often has God searched the earth for a leader willing to risk embarrassment, ridicule, or worse, only to be told "not now, God, not now"?

Boldness to do the right thing comes from practicing, moment-by-moment, an obedience to God's voice. It is hard work. It takes concentration. It demands the crucifixion of our immediate desires. It means we will not be concerned with what others think about us. It requires courage and faith in God's faithfulness.

The Rev. Joe Wright delivered the following prayer January 23, 1996, to the Kansas State House of

Representatives:

> *Heavenly Father, we come before you today to ask your forgiveness and seek Your direction and guidance. We know Your Word says, "Woe to those who call evil good," but that's exactly what we've done. We have lost our spiritual equilibrium and inverted our values.*
>
> *We confess that we have ridiculed the absolute truth of Your Word and called it pluralism.*
>
> *We have worshiped other gods and called it multiculturalism.*
>
> *We have endorsed perversion and called it an alternative lifestyle.*
>
> *We have exploited the poor and called it the lottery.*
>
> *We have neglected the needy and called it self-preservation.*
>
> *We have rewarded laziness and called it welfare.*
>
> *We have killed our unborn and called it choice.*
>
> *We have shot abortionists and called it justifiable.*
>
> *We have neglected to discipline our children and called it building esteem.*
>
> *We have abused power and called it political savvy.*
>
> *We have coveted our neighbor's possessions and called it ambition.*
>
> *We have polluted the air with profanity and pornography and called it freedom of expression.*
>
> *We have ridiculed the time-honored values of our forefathers and called it enlightenment.*

Search us, O God, and know our hearts today; try us and see if there be some wicked way in us: cleanse us from every sin and set us free. Guide and bless these men and women who have been sent here by the people of Kansas, and who have been ordained by You to govern this great state. Grant them Your wisdom to rule and may their decisions direct us to the center of Your will. I ask it in the name of Your Son, the living Savior, Jesus Christ. Amen.

LEADERSHIP IS ...

Leadership is character, not charisma. The story of Saul and David best models this. Saul was, by all accounts, tall, dark, and handsome. David was ruddy, gangly, and young when God called him. Saul had the personality to win people to his cause. David had the character to lead people in the direction God called him to lead. Saul was all about his needs. David was focused on obeying God.

Leadership has as its primary focus the raising up of other leaders whose primary goal should be to be ready and able to replace you. This is threatening to some. It should be motivating to all. If leadership is raising up leaders to replace itself, then the Lord will be free to grow the organization into the existing leadership. He will also move the available leadership into a new challenge that is just the perfect God-sized opportunity that is needed at that time. The natural corollary is: leadership demands faith.

The following insights have been taken ad hoc from the writings of John Maxwell's book, *Developing the Leaders Around You*.

1. Acquiring and keeping good people is the leader's most important task.

Leadership And Love

2. Those closest to the leader will determine the success level of that leader.
3. Grow a leader, grow the organization.
4. Everything rises and falls on leadership.
5. It takes a leader to know a leader, grow a leader, and show a leader.
6. There is no success without a successor.
7. The more people you lead, the more leaders you need.
8. A leader's success can be defined as the maximum utilization of the abilities of those under him.
9. Leaders must model the leadership they desire.
10. Lead (don't manage) the vision.
11. Do big things.
12. Spend more effort on the "Farm Team" than on the free agents.
13. Make difficult decisions.
14. Pay the price that attracts leaders.
15. To develop positive, successful people, look for the gold, not the dirt.
16. Character flaws cannot be ignored. They will eventually make a leader ineffective.
17. Leadership is influence.
18. People need to be trained and developed primarily in their areas of strength.
19. The growth and development of people is the highest calling of leadership.
20. Good leaders are good listeners.
21. Excellence breeds character, and character breeds excellence.

22. Care enough to confront.
23. Teams that don't bond can't build.
24. Respect must be earned over time; there are no shortcuts.
25. Delegation is the most powerful tool leaders have.[4]

Leadership is a foundational gift that starts the healthy process of God moving freely within the context of the body of Christ (1 Corinthians 12). Outstanding leaders are big dreamers. They believe in people and afford people ample opportunity to reach high enough to fail. Strong leaders provide security so that when they do stumble they see it as an opportunity, not a failure. Excellent leadership is always looking for ways to seek out and lift up new leaders to the cause God has called them to. Leadership is fundamental to the healthy operation of God's vision for the body of Christ. Leadership and love, for God's people, are inseparable.

CHAPTER five

Functional Excellence

THE BODY TOGETHER

In *The Man God Uses,* Henry and Tom Blackaby speak with clarity on the issue of the body of Christ.

> *Many people know the church is the body of Christ, but have no idea how that body functions. They may have some vague concept that the body of Christ should evangelize the world, feed the hungry, clothe the down-and-out, or meet together regularly to worship, but they don't know how they are to function within the body.*
>
> *God places the men He uses into bodies of believers for particular reasons. Just our acceptance of those who come in Jesus' name is something Jesus instructed us to do (read John 13:20). But, the concept of the body reinforces the need to reverence the truth of the gospel living in every believer. It is the truth that makes us one.*
>
> *With Christ as the head of the body, the rest is fitted together for a purpose God has in mind to impact the people around that body. Each man is strategically placed so that: 1) he can use his God-given gifts to equip and serve the body to maximize its impact in the*

community; and 2) he can be shaped and equipped by the rest of the body who use their God-given gifts for that purpose.

Each member of the body must perform his or her function in order for the body to work according to God's purposes. Each member impacts the rest of the members .... As far as I can tell, Christ has no other way to redeem a lost and spiritually decaying world except the Holy Spirit working through His body, the church. What are you currently doing in His church? How are you using the gifts God has given you to equip His saints for ministry?

> And He Himself gave some to be apostles, some prophets, some evangelists, and some pastors and teachers, for the equipping of the saints for the work of ministry, for the edifying of the body of Christ, till we all come to the unity of the faith and of the knowledge of the Son of God, to a perfect man, to the measure of the stature of the fullness of Christ... but, speaking the truth in love, may grow up in all things into Him who is the head—Christ—from whom the whole body, joined and knit together by what every joint supplies, according to the effective working by which every part does its share, causes growth of the body for the edifying of itself in love.
>
> Ephesians 4:11–13, 15–16

Do you see the importance of using your talents and gifts to build up the body of Christ, to prepare and equip its members for works of service, to promote unity and love between members in your church under Christ's leadership?

If you want to know what a church looks like that does not follow these guidelines, look at the story of Ananias and Saphira (see Acts 5:1–11) to see how God treats those in His church who are consumed by selfish desires. Look to the result of Achan's sin of covetousness (see Joshua 7: 22:25) and how it affected the whole community. The Israelite army was routed at Ai, and many people died because of Achan's secret disobedience to God's commands. Look to see what Christ has to say to His churches in Revelation 2–3. Many in the church had lost their first love and followed after their own immoral desires. When members of the body are dysfunctional in their roles, the entire body is compromised in its usefulness and effectiveness in God's kingdom. Each functions "according to the grace that is given to us" (Romans 12:6). Do not receive the grace of God in vain! (see 2 Corinthians 6:1).

The church works together under the leadership of Christ as the Head to accomplish mighty and amazing feats through His power and leadership. A church that functions properly as a body of Christ will be characterized by several things.

1. *Members care for one another, in love, and carry each other's burdens.*

2. *Members equip, encourage, undergird, and protect one another with the Holy Spirit's help.*

3. *Members do together through the power of Christ what they could not possibly do alone.*

4. *Members serve as Christ's hands, feet, and messengers, impacting communities, countries, and the world.*

5. *Members become living bodies of Christ, demonstrating the nature and character of Christ for all to see.*

6. *Members are obedient to the Father, and He will use them to carry out His mission to take the gospel to*

> *every person in every area of the world. Christ will live out His life obeying the Father, through His people, to continue His mission of redemption and reconciliation.*
>
> 7. *Members continue to grow, mature, and reproduce themselves as a church in other places. The church has offspring by planting other churches.*[5]

The Christian school, when made up of Christ's believers, is the body of Christ. In fact, the Christian school is the church come alive. Too often today's church would argue that the Christian school, though a ministry, is not to "compete" with the church. What a pity! The Christian school *is* the church. If God has called the school into existence, then the fruit will bear this out.

The Christian school leader must recognize the importance of the biblical model of a healthy body working together. The best leaders understand that to be a good leader you need to be a good follower. Jesus must always be the focal point of all leadership decisions. First time obedience by the leader to Christ is essential. Every leader must understand the importance of the following maxim taken from the teachings of Arlin Horton, President of ABEKA books and Pensacola Christian College:

"To be in authority, you must first be under authority."[6]

Balance—the Great Equalizer

In too many Christian organizations, the strong gift of one or a few persons are elevated above the gifts of others to the detriment of the ministry and surrounding community. In one particular Christian school, over the course of a number of years, the idea that technology was important grew from a God-breathed passion from a leader with the gift of administration into a man-made obsession. A school that once preached "the Word" in every class morphed into a type of country prep school, where the pressure from parents for increasing academic excellence eclipsed the focus on Jesus. Academic excellence is a legitimate goal, but never to the detriment of Christian ideals. In fact, academic strength and a focus on Jesus are closely related, not mutually exclusive.

The following parable illustrates what happened to the vibrant Christian school and may happen again elsewhere if Christian school leaders are not in touch with the will of God. This illustration comes from the Horizon Christian Fellowship Discipleship training package.

On a dangerous sea coast where shipwrecks often occur there was once a crude little life-saving station. The building was just a hut, and there was only one boat, but the few devoted members kept a constant watch over the sea, and with no thought for themselves went out day and night tirelessly searching for the lost. Some of those who were saved, and various others in the surrounding area, wanted to become associated with the station and give of their time and money and effort for the support of its work. New boats were brought and new crews trained. The little life-saving station grew.

Some of the members of the life-saving station were unhappy that the building was so crude, and so poorly equipped. They felt that a more comfortable place should be provided as the first refuge of those saved from the sea. They replaced the emergency cots with beds and put better furniture in the enlarged building. Now the life-saving station became a popular gathering place for its members, and they decorated it beautifully and furnished it exquisitely, because they used it as a sort of club. Fewer members were now interested in going to sea on life-saving missions, so they hired life-boat crews to do this work. The life-saving motif still prevailed in this club's decoration, and there was a liturgical life-boat in the room where the club initiations were held. About this time a large ship was wrecked off the coast. The hired crews brought in boat loads of cold, wet and half-drowned people. They were dirty and sick and some of them had black skin and some had yellow skin. The beautiful new club was in chaos. So the property committee immediately had a shower house built inside the club where victims of shipwrecks could be cleaned up before coming inside.

At the next meeting, there was a split in the club membership. Most of the members wanted to stop the club's life-saving activities as being unpleasant and a hindrance to the normal social life of the club. Some members insisted upon life-saving as their primary purpose and pointed out that they were still called a life-saving station. But they were finally voted down and told that if they wanted to save the lives of all the various kinds of people who were shipwrecked in those waters, they could begin their own life-saving station down the coast. They did.

As the years went by, the new station experienced the same changes that had occurred in the old. It evolved into a club, and yet another life-saving station was founded. History continued to repeat itself, and if you visit that sea coast today, you will find a number of exclusive clubs along that shore. Shipwrecks are frequent in those waters, but most people drown.

In a particular Christian school down South, in a pattern all too familiar worldwide, an administrator's gift for preaching and evangelizing becomes so dominant that other gifts such as mercy, help, hospitality, and the like are pushed aside. The school then begins to suffer from a perceived lack of love and compassion. The simple solution is to encourage all the gifts of the body to work as one, not alone. It is leadership's responsibility to ensure the balance is attained. Leadership and love must be synonymous.

I recall with sterling clarity a time when the gifts of the body of Christ working together saved my ministry and my sanity. I had just arrived as the new headmaster of a small Christian school system (pre-K to twelve). I had come under enormous and bitter personal attack. Since I was new and had moved over 3,000 miles to answer the call, I had no idea who was friend or foe. I soon found out on both counts.

In one case, our business bookkeeper came to me, and with the gift of prophecy told me the Lord was in the midst of "separating sheep from sheep and goats from goats" (Ezekiel 34:17). This was not only comforting, but also hugely enlightening. Up until that time, the Enemy had been doing a number on me through doubt, confusion, and guilt. From that moment on, I had direction to pray that God would move swiftly and bring great "unity, harmony and love" in the place of gossip, lies, and anger.

It was during this time of horrifying attack that I first experienced the true gift of mercy in my life. I was attending a Grandparent's Day celebration when I was surrounded by the father and family of a woman on staff who was both vocal and demonic in her attempts to discredit me and have me fired. This father was an ex-Marine and made it quite clear what he would do to me if I continued to run the school as stated. At one point, he actually threatened me with bodily harm, and worse. His daughter, the renegade teacher, watched with glee from an office window as I was intimidated and harassed.

This particular attack had come on the heels of tremendous pressure from a group of teachers and parents in cahoots to have me ousted. The crux of their complaint was that we were focusing too much on Jesus. The notion that a Christian school would boldly proclaim the gospel of Christ was too much for them to bear. God had called me to refocus the vision of the school, "... that in all things He may have the preeminence" (Colossians 1:18). The cost of doing this was too much for them to bear.

I was weepy, hurt, saddened, and, most of all, frustrated with the Lord. Why had I been called to such a dreadful ministry? I had come from a school that was growing by leaps and bounds, had a vibrant track record, and employed a loving and nurturing team dedicated to serving the Lord. I could not believe that Christians could be so mean, bitter, vicious, and manipulative. I felt like I was in a bad dream that kept moving in slow motion ... backward.

As I reentered the school after being threatened by the Marine father, people coming and going jammed me up at the front door. I had the sharpest pit in my stomach. My face felt like it would stretch all the way from my head to my toes. I was in a daze. Then, out of the blue, it happened.

I was twirled around twice, hugged from three angles, given a kiss on the cheek, and the sweetest words I had heard in a long time flowed through my ears: "Chapin, I love you and I am praying for you." The woman had gray-blue hair, was in her sixties, and was the wife of our retiring lower campus administrator. I was stunned. I had not felt true undeserved kindness and grace in a long time. I was a very unpopular person out on "the street." Why was she so kind to me?

She looked me square in the eye and said "I'm not the only one who believes what you are doing is God's will. You follow Jesus and let Him take care of the rest of it." I know my mouth was open at that door as hundreds of people filtered by. She looked once more at me, smiled the warmest smile a belittled fellow could ask for, gave me another hug, and said "I know God called you here because I prayed for you to come." As she left to go round up her husband or grandchildren she shouted "keep up the great work, Chapin, keep up the great work." Thank God she exercised her God-given gifts when she did; it strengthened me in a time of great challenge.

There was another time when, as headmaster, I was beginning the planning process for the next school year. The administrative team was solid though still trying to mesh our gifts. Each person loved Jesus and wanted to serve the Lord. It was a terrific surprise when a woman in our office called me in and said the Lord told her to tell me to "watch my back." I listened, prayed for discernment, and really thought nothing more of it. Until …

One of our administrators decided that he had been called by God to begin a new work in a town not too far away. In so doing we sent him off with our sincerest blessings. We offered whatever resources we had to help him get started. He took us up on a teacher or two, some supplies, lots of ideas and the like. What would have surprised me (but didn't, because of the prophetic warning) was that he was also spreading false and misleading information about the school. The irony is that this was unnecessary. It simply reflected his lack of confidence and his fears. I praised God for warning me, though I did little with the information until after the fact.

Here is one other instance of God using the body to minister to me as an administrator. I had been going through a terrible time of not receiving the forgiveness of the Lord in my life. I was wracked with intermittent guilt and anguish. This, in turn, produced a type of paralysis in my faith. I was in bondage. It was painful and depressing.

The registrar came to me one day, smiled and said, "Let's talk spiritual things. God has a special delivery just for you." I was all ears. She continued, "You have had a breakthrough in the area of forgiveness of self. No longer will Satan use your past to lord it over you. God is preparing you for this awesome blessing and responsibility at His school. The Scripture for you is, "And I also say to you that you are Peter, and on this rock I will build My church, and the gates of Hades shall not prevail against it" (Matthew 16:18).

I was relieved in a very physical as well as spiritual way. In each of these instances and dozens more I had a choice to make. I could brush off the "lesser" gifts as "flaky," "weird," "inappropriate," or worse. I learned early in the ministry that I was called by God to exhort each person in his or her gift, even if I didn't understand it. That decision alone has sustained me through exhilarating growth in the ministry and devastating disappointment. The true moral of this lesson is to encourage and use the gifts God has placed in the ministry around you. It is ultimately for your protection and edification.

Vision

The Bible is clear, "Where there is no revelation (vision), the people cast off restraint; but happy is he who keeps the law" (Proverbs 29:18). No vision, know chaos. Organizations that live off a cult of personality, or "old manna," are doomed in the long run. Christian schools, like any healthy organization, must continually reinvent themselves. The trick is to maintain the integrity of the ancient landmarks while moving forward with a whole heart into the next stage of development as the Lord leads.

Leadership is fundamentally about vision. A leader cannot function without God-breathed vision. When a leader stops having vision for the ministry, he becomes a manager. The school then needs to very quickly find a leader with vision. Too often Christian schools atrophy under the well-intentioned administration of those who are comfortable and content. Jesus was always moving forward. Jesus is our foremost example of a leader full of vision.

GOD'S WILL

One of the most difficult aspects of leadership is determining the Lord's will. To be sure, God speaks clearly in prayer, through the Bible, in circumstances, within relationships, and so forth. It is usually not God who has the problem. In most cases we have missed what the Lord is doing because of our "lust of the flesh, lust of the eyes, or pride of life." In some cases, the Devil is working overtime. Here is a concise word of encouragement in the area of God's will. Be encouraged!

> Lift your eyes now look from the place where you are—northward, southward, eastward and westward; for all the land which you see I give to you and your descendents forever.
>
> Genesis 13:14–15

No desire will ever be placed in you by the Holy Spirit unless He intends to fulfill it. So let your faith rise up and soar away to claim all the land you can discover. Joshua understood this as God told him; "every place that the sole of your foot will tread upon I have given you ..." (Joshua 1:3). Remember, God does the heavy lifting, we just need to abide in Him and walk where he instructs us to go. Great news!

Everything you can comprehend through faith's vision belongs to you. Look as far as you can, for it is all yours. All you long to be as a Christian, and all you long to do for God, are within the possibilities of faith. Then draw closer to Him, and with your Bible before you, and your soul completely open to the power of the Spirit, allow your entire being to receive the baptism of His presence. As He opens your understanding, enabling you to see His fullness, believe He has it all for you. Accept for yourself all the promises of His Word, all the desires He awakens within you, and all the possibilities of what you could become as a follower of Jesus. All the land you see is given to you.

The provision of His grace, which helps us along the way to the fulfillment of His promise, is actually tied to the inner vision God has given us. He who puts the natural instinct in the heart of a bird to fly across a continent in search of a warmer climate is too good to deceive it. Just as we are confident He placed the instinct within the bird, we can be assured He has also provided balmy breezes and spring-like sun to meet it when it arrives.

And He who breathes heavenly hope into our hearts will not deceive or fail us when we press forward toward its realization.

So they went and found it just as He had said to them

Luke 22:13[7]

CHAPTER
six

Fundamentals of Excellence

Philosophy

The Christian school must develop specific philosophies for core operational areas. The reason a philosophy of operational objectives is so important is because it helps delineate the school's distinctive qualities. It also keeps the school from going down rabbit trails or dead ends. A philosophy of ministry in every operational area helps unify the entire ministry. It also streamlines decision making. Examples of operational areas in need of strong philosophies are school vision, mission statement, school purpose, statement of faith, and school objectives. I include examples in each area to provide strong, conservative, God-centered ideas for those reading this in search of clarity in these all-important areas.

Vision

Christian school leadership in general is initiated via the board and headmaster. The board, in conjunction with the headmaster, selects God's vision for the school. This vision statement is the first and most important document the leadership approves. The vision statement directs all other decisions within the school. An example of a simple yet compelling vision statement is "that in all things He may have the preeminence" (Colossians 1:8).

Mission Statement

The mission statement is the second document to be approved. The mission statement is developed through the lens of the vision statement. The mission statement expands the vision. It is designed to elaborate on the vision in a practical manner. An example of a well integrated mission statement is: "Your Christian school exists to help prepare children to be disciples of the Lord Jesus Christ. The school seeks to train children academically, physically, emotionally, and spiritually—thoroughly equipping them for every good work (2 Timothy 3:17). Your Christian school works in partnership with parents and local churches to attain this goal."

School Purpose

The school purpose is the third document to be approved. Again, the vision of the school directs its purpose. The purpose statement is an action document. Heavy verb usage characterizes the purpose statement's language. The purpose should include broad spiritual, academic, physical, and emotional goals. An example of a well written purpose statement is:

Your Christian school:
- Serves the community in the name of our Lord Jesus Christ in providing loving Christian care and high quality Christian education for children and concerned parents.
- Provides a full educational curriculum developing the

spiritual, mental, social, and physical facets of the child's personality and character.

- Excites the child with the learning experience and takes full advantage of a child's natural desire to learn.
- Serves God by instilling a desire and love for Christ in each child so that he / she will want to exemplify Him in all areas of life. Likewise, it gives to the child a quality education designed to show that man's knowledge is a reflection of God's plan.

STATEMENT OF FAITH

The statement of faith is the fourth document to be addressed. The statement of faith is very specific. It covers the beliefs the leadership specifically holds to be foundational to the existence of the school. Anyone working at the school must believe and uphold all the views in this document, or seek employment elsewhere. An example of a sound statement of faith is:

We believe:

1. in one God, the Creator and Sustainer of the universe, eternally existent in three persons: Father, Son, and Holy Spirit;
2. in the divine inspiration, infallibility, and final authority of the Bible as the Word of God;
3. in the uniqueness of man, by virtue of his special creation in God's image, and his responsibility to understand and master the world to the glory of God;
4. in the unique deity of the Lord Jesus Christ, the incarnate, virgin-born Son of God;
5. in the representative and substitutionary death of our Lord Jesus Christ as the necessary atonement for our sins;

6. in the resurrection of the crucified body of our Lord and that blessed hope, His personal return;
7. in the power of the Holy Spirit in the work of regeneration and His continuing work in the heart of the believer;
8. in the bodily resurrection of the just and the unjust, the everlasting blessedness of the saved, and the everlasting punishment of the lost;
9. in the spiritual unity of believers in our Lord Jesus Christ;
10. in the heterosexual marriage relationship as the only God ordained family system.

SCHOOL OBJECTIVES

Finally, the school objectives are the natural outgrowth of the vision, mission statement, purpose, and statement of faith. This document should be specific and should promote easy assessment. An example of this is as follows.

Spiritually, the school endeavors to:

- help establish each student's faith in God as Creator, Redeemer, and Provider;
- teach the Bible and develop a love and respect for it;
- help the student develop a biblical worldview by integrating life and studies with the Bible;
- encourage the student to live a life of obedience and excellence for the glory of God;
- develop within the student a servant's heart;

Socially, the school endeavors to:

- develop the student's personality, based on biblical concepts, to the fullest potential of his / her capabilities;
- teach students to respect and protect all human life;

- promote a biblical view of time, work, and material possessions;
- develop responsible citizenship ideals and encourage active participation in all areas of community life and government;
- encourage local church membership and service;
- understand the principles established by God within relationships;

Physically, the school endeavors to:

- teach respect for the human body as the temple of the Holy Spirit;
- develop fine and gross motor skills;
- instill proper dietary habits;
- offer a well-planned physical education program that promotes lifelong fitness and health habits.

Academically, the school endeavors to:

- promote high academic standards by helping each student realize his / her full academic potential;
- provide each student with a course of study in the fundamental processes used in communicating reading, writing, speaking, listening, and mathematics;
- teach and encourage the use of good study skills;
- develop the student's ability to think critically, creatively, and constructively;
- motivate each student to be an independent and lifelong learner;
- encourage discussion on current events in the community, the nation, and the world;
- promote a desire in each student to fulfill the cultural mandate of captivating all areas of culture and nature

for the honor of Christ;

- create an understanding and appreciation of various world cultures through cultural and social studies and the teaching of a foreign language;
- engender an appreciation of the fine arts through music classes, art instruction, and humanities classes;
- train students in the use of computers to enhance core subjects and provide skills for word processing, programming, and creative expression;
- teach basic and advanced math facts, concepts, and skills, and to demonstrate life application for math;
- challenge students to study God's creation through science;
- Provide classic children's literature for reading and discussion;
- encourage a love of reading and creative writing;
- promote the discipline of logical thinking and research.

Practical Implementation

In terms of integration of philosophy through operational areas, let me provide a few helpful hints. First, once you arrive at the distinctive philosophy for your ministry, this philosophy will guide you through difficult or controversial decisions with clarity and purpose. Second, do not, under any circumstance, change a philosophy statement in the middle of a difficult decision. The temptation is to second-guess and manipulate circumstances to fit the issue. Wrong! Don't do it. The integrity of the ministry will falter if you do. People will lose confidence, or worse, they will no longer care about the ministry.

Remember to first establish operational philosophies.

Then go about decision-making within the respective areas of operations, with the school philosophies as a type of template. Examples of controversial, but necessary, areas of operational decision making include the following: ministry focus, spiritual emphasis, behavior / discipline, academic thrust, curriculum, tuition, salary and benefits, dress code. I will discuss three of the aforementioned operational areas in order to flesh out the importance of establishing philosophies in the Christian school prior to making decisions.

The areas covered will be behavior / discipline, curriculum, tuition, salary and benefits.

CHAPTER seven

Standards of Excellence

BEHAVIOR / DISCIPLINE

Clear, consistent, and prayerful implementation of a well-written behavior / discipline program is the most important operational aspect of a well run Christian school. The Christian school that neglects this area may quickly witness (1) loss of its best faculty, (2) the withdrawal of the brightest children and (3) a sense of apathy and despair settling upon the entire proceedings. Develop a strong expectation for discipline / behavior in the school and then execute it each and every day with a passion reserved for preparing for the D-day invasion!

"This is totally ridiculous! I'm not even sure I want my child to attend this school anymore!" the mother shouted over the hushed tones of a parent meeting in early February. Other parents silently fumed in their seats, waiting to pounce on the slightest weakness in the response. I waited, smiled, and looked squarely into the eyes of the mother posing the charge. "Ma'am, I want to be very clear," I began. "I will not discuss the specifics of any discipline case outside the context of meetings with children and their parents. I will say, though, that we are administering the discipline policy as per the student handbook. We are doing what we said we would do."

"Don't you think what you are doing is too harsh?" the lioness threatened. "What if it was your child? Where is the grace? I am so glad Jesus doesn't treat you and me like you are treating this young child. You are heartless, and we have lost the heart of what this school was founded on because of you!" she spewed forth. She then looked for approval and sat down.

"Thank you for your concern," I began. "I want you to know we do not administer discipline arbitrarily in this school. We spent three months last spring in committees discussing every part of our school handbook. The question of zero tolerance was noted as a philosophical position with strong expectations, requiring even stronger consistency in administering it in the event of an infraction. As you recall, every parent and every child received a handbook in the summer, and had time to read it, pose questions, and sign the contract stating that they would support the school and its policies and procedures." I paused.

"In any instance of zero tolerance the handbook requires an immediate 9 week expulsion from school," I continued. "The school's philosophy states that it is a privilege to attend Christian school. Every member of the school community is personally responsible for his actions and their consequences. Individuals have a responsibility to make good choices. The school does not buy into the secular mindset that everyone's rights supercede their responsibilities. In the event a child makes a poor choice resulting in suspension, expulsion or even lunch clean up, the school will lovingly and consistently administer the consequences outlined in the handbook. It's that simple."

The silence in the room was deafening. It was the first time in this school that the leadership had a clear and emphatic direction for school discipline. The expectations for behavior were high. Trash-free bathroom floors, clean and uncluttered halls and aisles, tidy cafeteria, well-organized bulletin boards, halls with well designed posters. These all played a part in establishing a strong behavioral expectation.

The most powerful component of the behavioral / discipline program was its day-to-day implementation in the classroom and the offices. Teachers were instructed to hold children accountable for daily homework. A missed homework assignment resulted in a note sent home. Three notes resulted in a session of Saturday school. Instead of after-school detentions, students came to Saturday school from 7:00 a.m. until noon. They sat in a classroom and were allowed to read the Bible or do homework. The rules in Saturday school stated no sleeping, no heads down, no communicating of any kind. If a student broke these rules, he was required to attend an additional two weeks of Saturdays. One twenty-minute break halfway through the morning was the only opportunity for chitchat.

In cases of disruptive behavior teachers are instructed to send a child outside the classroom into the hall. The administration is expected to "sweep" the halls once a period. The administrator gives a child caught outside the classroom firm instructions, which include identifying and taking responsibility for one's actions. The administrative focus is to back up, *not undermine*, the teacher's decision. The child knows there is no possibility of "splitting the defense." The teacher's decision is law. The administrator, acting as court of appeals, upholds the teacher's decisions.

It normally takes one solid semester of consistent implementation by the faculty and administration to begin turning the tide of slothfulness in studies, disruption in classes, and malignant influences from society through Christian students. The fruit of a strong behavior / discipline strategy is peace. The Bible tells fathers to discipline their children, and they will have peace. Additionally, a collegial atmosphere develops within the faculty and administrative team. Always be consistent. Always be truthful and tender as unto the Lord.

The effectiveness of the school behavior / discipline program skyrockets once a teacher or administrator publicly admits a mistake when they make one. The tendency is to move on to save face or whatever. Big mistake! Children are very intuitive. When appropriate, let them know that you made a wrong call and are trying to make it right. Watch your school go to a new level with the Lord, as leadership humbles itself in the presence of the Lord.

Included here are two very effective discipline codes merged from experience and many administrative meetings. The first deals exclusively with grades K through five. The second is designed for sixth through twelfth grades. In every case, parents are required to sign and return the Parent / Student Handbook Agreement.

Parent / Student Handbook Agreement

One Lord, one school, one campus

Parental and Student Agreement

Parent and student applicants must agree to and sign the following parental statement:

1. I appreciate the standards of the school and do not tolerate profanity, obscenity in word or action, dishonor to God and the Word of God, or disrespect to the personnel of this school. Therefore, I agree to support all regulations of the school in the applicant's behalf and authorize this school to employ such discipline, as it deems wise for the training of my child.

2. I agree to uphold and support the high academic standard of the school by providing a place at home for my child to study and giving my child encouragement in the completion of homework and assignments.

3. I understand that my child's needs must fit the educational capabilities of the school.

4. I promise to pay my financial obligations to the school on the dates due and understand that it may be necessary to withdraw my child if prior acceptable arrangements are not made on a past due account. I also understand only tuition paid in advance is refundable in the event of withdrawal during the school year.

5. I give permission for my child to take part in all school activities and school sponsored trips away from the school premises, and absolve the school from liability to me or my child at school or during any school activity.

6. I understand that the school reserves the right to dismiss any child who fails to comply with the established regulations and discipline or whose financial obligation remains unpaid.

7. I understand that the school is an extension of the family and the parent and teacher are co-workers in the child's education. I will contact the teacher and discuss any areas of concern before discussing the problem with others. I will encourage and support my child's teacher.

Sign and return by September 8, 2005

Parent / Student Handbook Agreement

    I have personally read, understood, and agree to the guidelines contained in the *Salisbury Christian School*

Handbook. While enrolled in SCS, I agree to cooperate with these standards to the fullest extent.

Student / Date

As a parent I have read the *Salisbury Christian School* Handbook. I will cooperate with the school in its endeavor to maintain these high Christian standards.

Parent / Date

* This agreement letter must be signed by both student and parent and returned to the school by Friday, September 8, 2005. No student will be allowed to attend class without returning this completed form to the school office.

p. 3 LC handbook

SCHOOL CULTURE / DISCIPLINE POLICY AND PROCEDURES

Biblical Guidelines

He who disdains instruction despises his own soul, But he who heeds rebuke gets understanding.

Proverbs 15:32

My son, do not despise the chastening of the Lord, Nor detest His correction; For whom the Lord loves He corrects, Just as a father the son in whom he delights.

Proverbs 3:11–12

One of the most important lessons for any student to learn is how to properly respond to all authority: their parents, school personnel, other authority figures, and most importantly, God. In order to accomplish this goal, we must set discipline standards that are enforced fairly, consistently, and lovingly.

However, discipline is never a cut and dried step-by-step procedure. It is important to remember that we are dealing with different personalities with different needs. For this reason, the teacher and administration must rely closely on the wisdom and leading of the Holy Spirit in specific situations.

We will encourage students to be ambassadors for Christ; not only at school and school related activities, but also at home and in the larger community. We recognize that Christlike behavior does not result from following a list of dos and don'ts, but rather from one's acceptance of Christ as Lord and Savior and allowing the Holy Spirit to enter one's life and take charge of every aspect of it. The intent of this section is to offer students a model of a Christian lifestyle that honors God in their school, home, and community.

Those who follow the teaching of the Lord Jesus Christ are self-disciplined. Parents are commanded to follow these teachings.

> And you, fathers, do not provoke your children to wrath, but bring them up in the training and admonition of the Lord.
>
> Ephesians 6:4

Although discipline is not always pleasant, it is an essential aspect of godly education in the home and in the Christian school.

> Now no chastening seems to be joyful for the present, but painful; nevertheless, afterward it yields the peaceable fruit of righteousness to those who have been trained by it.
>
> Hebrews 12:11

SCS stands with the parents of the students in the ministry of nurturing Disciples of Christ. Without becoming legalistic in our expectations, *SCS* has developed certain principles in which we will train our students. These basic principles are derived from God's Word.

Study and be prepared:

I Thessalonians 4:11 ...that you also aspire to lead a quiet life, to mind your own business, and to work with your own hands, as we commanded you.

Proverbs 14:23a In all labor there is profit.

Proverbs 23:12 Apply your heart to instruction, And your ears to words of knowledge.

Speak kindly and in turn

Ephesians 4:32 And be kind to one another, tenderhearted, forgiving one another, even as God in Christ forgave you.

James 1:19 Everyone should be quick to listen, slow to speak and slow to anger.

Proverbs 21:23 He who guards his mouth and tongue keeps himself from calamity.

Be kind and respect all those in authority over you

2 Timothy 2:23-24 Don't have anything to do with foolish and stupid arguments, because you know they produce quarrels. And the Lord's servant must be kind to everyone, able to teach, not resentful.

Colossians 4:6 Let your speech always be with grace, seasoned with salt, that you may know how you ought to answer each one.

I Peter 5:5 Likewise you younger people, submit yourselves to your elders. Yes, all of you be submissive to one another, and be clothed with humility, for "God resists the proud, But gives grace to the humble."

Respect other's property

Leviticus 19:13 You shall not cheat your neighbor, nor rob him.

Philippians 2:3 Let nothing be done through selfish ambition or conceit, but in lowliness of mind let each esteem others better than himself.

Romans 13:9–10b You shall love your neighbor as yourself. Love does no harm to a neighbor.

In all things, do your best

Ephesians 2:10 For we are His workmanship, created in Christ Jesus for good works, which God prepared beforehand that we should walk in them.

Colossians 3:17 And whatever you do in word or deed, do all in the name of the Lord Jesus, giving thanks to God the Father through Him.

Serve one another

Ephesians 4:16b Serve one another in love.

Ephesians 6:7 … with goodwill doing service, as to the Lord, and not to men.

School Culture

Students will profit and find satisfaction from school life by adopting a positive attitude and by following the rules designed to provide safety, order, and a productive educational atmosphere. We believe modeling values is teaching values. Our school culture items help establish the right kinds of values early in our children's minds. The values we espouse are not arbitrary. They are time-honored, true, and "other-centered." Our school culture items are as follows:

1. No hats on heads in any room after coming in from outside.
2. Dress for success: Students are asked to wear their finest clothes on days when they are representing the Lord, their family, and their school through *SCS* sports, the arts, music, etc. It is requested that the boys wear slacks and a tie, and girls wear dresses.

3. Ladies first: Boys will be encouraged to defer (let girls go first) to ladies when entering a room.
4. Speaker's delight: Students will be encouraged to stand for the first adult speaker and any guest that may address the school.
5. Stand and deliver: Students are encouraged to stand when addressing an adult in class, when asking a question, reciting, etc. This builds posture, confidence, and sets a strong learning message.
6. Honor code: Students are exhorted to commit to honor and integrity by never allowing theft, cheating, gossip, or other wrong behavior to occur, first in their own lives, and second, by those persons around them. Students are exhorted to follow Matthew 18 in all interpersonal problem areas. Students are exhorted to humbly submit to God and voluntarily seek counsel from others in leadership if they have personal problems. If a student is involved in and / or witnesses any behavior contrary to the standards set forth in the handbook, he / she is to report it to the administration as soon as possible. If a student chooses to withhold any information, then he / she is running the risk for being disciplined by the school for withholding truth.
7. Class ambassadors: Each class will have a student designated to greet guests at the door, introduce him / herself, the teacher, and class, shake hands, ask for prayer requests and seek to answer questions the visitors may have.
8. Pledge to the American flag, Christian flag, and God's Word daily near the beginning of the day.
9. Love one another!

Parental Support

All disciplinary decisions are made prayerfully. It is of utmost importance that the parents support the teacher and / or the administration in matters of discipline. If a disagreement arises in the corrective measures taken, a parent should not voice that disagreement to the child until after speaking with the teacher or administrator. Oftentimes, only one perspective is represented. It is important, however, that we teach the children, through our own example, to submit to the authority established by God.

General School Rules for Students

1. Parents must use discretion in allowing students to bring personal items for sharing. The school will not be responsible for replacement or repair costs of items brought from home. It is requested that the following items not be brought without permission from the child's teacher: electronic equipment and games, baseballs, softball, hockey sticks and pucks, rollerblades, skateboards, and other items not permitted in class directed activities.

2. Throwing rocks, dirt, sand, or other harmful objects is strictly forbidden.

3. Students must obtain permission from the teacher or assistant before leaving the classroom or playground.

4. Students are not allowed to leave campus for any reason without permission from the office and parents.

5. Students must remain in the designated supervised playground area during recess.

6. All play and school equipment must be used safely and properly only in the manner for which it was designed.

7. Students arriving after 8:30 a.m. must go to the office for an "Admit to Class" slip.

8. Name calling, teasing, and bullying will not be tolerated.

Minor and Major Infractions

Besides the general school rules, students may also be disciplined for the following Infractions. These violations will be referred to as either minor or major infractions.

Minor infractions:

    Disobedience • Dress code violation

    Inappropriate language • Unkindness

    Disrespect • Inappropriate behavior •

    Talking / calling out • Unprepared • Inappropriate attitude

Major infractions:

    Fighting, physical harassment / threats • Cursing / swearing

    Repeated teasing / name calling • Using God's name in vain

    Gossip / slander • Stealing, cheating, lying

    Deliberate disobedience / disrespect

    Possession of a weapon • Vandalism / graffiti

    Repetition of minor infractions • Scornful attitude

Classroom Discipline Guideline

Classroom discipline requires two components: Preventative discipline and corrective discipline.

Preventative:

Each teacher will devise his or her own system of motivation on an individual and class level. This plan will consist of verbal praise, awards, privileges, treats, a trip to the principal, and / or class parties. The purpose is to encourage proper behavior in all students.

Corrective:

It is our goal that the teacher, administration, and parents present a united front to the student in the spirit of helping the child. Since the teacher / administration works closely with the children during class time when parents are usually not present, they will need to handle situations when a child displays inappropriate behavior. Though each individual teacher devises their own structure of discipline, the following will be recommended to the teachers by the administration as a possible structure. It is taken from the four categories of individuals in the book of Proverbs.

The wise:

- Thinking God's thoughts and acting God's way
- We become wise by consistently making wise choices
- Acting as Jesus would act
- Thinking as Jesus would think
- *Scripture: Proverbs 4:7, Luke 2:52, James 1:5, Psalm 51:6, Ecclesiastes 2:26*

The simple:

- A follower ... a very gullible person
- Is easily deceived by others
- Can't see the trouble or consequences that are coming
- God's Word will make this person wise and help him not to believe all he sees or hears
- *Scripture: Proverbs 14:15, 13:20, 22:3, 19:25, 21:11, 9:4–6*

The foolish:

- Doesn't see anything wrong with what she is doing

- Enjoys getting into mischief ... Must be corrected
- Brings grief and sorrow to his parents
- Quick to quarrel ... Quick tempered
- Does not flee temptation ... she thinks what she is doing is right
- *Scripture: Proverbs 10:23, 17:25, 10:1, 19:13, 15:20, 29:11, 14:16*

The scorner / mocker:

- Bad attitude, angry, disgusted
- Sometimes passive / aggressive in the use of body language
- Dislikes and does not listen to those who correct him
- Causes quarrels and strife
- Wants to solve problems herself, not God's way
- *Scripture: Proverbs 15:12, 13:1, 22:10, 24:9, 14:6*

Each teacher will use the following plan to design his own classroom consequence structure. The student will begin in the wise column, but will be moved down with each infraction. This would be done on a daily basis with student's starting the day with a clean record. This plan could be implemented by the use of a Student chart.

Wise: Hooray!	*Thinking God's ways and acting like Jesus*
Simple: Warning	*Making simple mistakes—think first!*
Foolish: Parent Communication (PC)	*Not thinking or acting God's way*
Scornful: Administrative Referral	*Going against God*

Administrative Referrals and Course of Action

The administration reserves the right to discipline every

case based on its unique and special nature. A child may be referred to the administration for disciplinary correction for one of three reasons:

1. Reaching a final consequence as set by the teacher (usually for minor infractions)
2. Severe clause (major infractions)
3. Prayer / counseling

An administrative referral for minor infractions will *generally* result in the following (per semester):

First infraction	CTR
Second infraction	CTR, call to parents
Third infraction	CTR, call to parents, parent communication
Fourth infraction	CTR, call to parents, Saturday school
Fifth infraction	Treated as first major infractions

An administrative referral for major infractions will generally result in the following disciplinary actions per semester (but are not limited to the following):

First infraction	CTR, call to parents, Saturday school
Second infraction	CTR, suspension until parent conference, (teacher, principal, parents)
Third infraction	CTR, one to three days suspension
Fourth infraction	CTR, three to five days suspension
Fifth infraction	Behavioral probation and contract

In certain cases, a disciplinary action may result in an immediate suspension of one to five days (or longer: see Expulsions #2). *SCS* reserves the right to automatically suspend any student from school whose behavior or attitude disrupts the tranquility and culture of the school. *Attendance at SCS is a privilege, not a right.* (In the event that the nature of a specific infraction relates *more* to those usually dealt with at the middle / high school level, *SCS* will follow the disciplinary measures stated in the *SCS* Middle / High Handbook.)

Clarification on Specific Course of Actions

Counsel / teach correct behavior / aid in reconciliation

We are all-responsible for our own sins and are in need of repentance. It is wonderful to know that there is true forgiveness through Jesus Christ! However, there are many different motives for sin.... Sometimes even painful emotional experiences result in very inappropriate behavior. Therefore, it is the intention of the administration to shepherd the heart of your child. This will include active listening, teaching correct behavior, and aiding the child in reconciliation with others as well as with Jesus.

Saturday school

Saturday school will be a part of the consequences for major infractions of third through fifth graders. The parent(s) will decide the date that it will be served (within a three week period of the infraction). The students are required to be at the school from 7:00 a.m.–9:30 a.m. Lateness will result in an additional Saturday school (no exceptions).

Parent conference with administrator

Parent Conferences will always begin and end with prayer for wisdom and discernment in regard to the issue of discussion. The principles of conflict resolution and Matthew 18:15–16 will be followed.

Suspension

> Now no chastening seems to be joyful for the present, but painful; nevertheless, afterward it yields the peaceable fruit of righteousness to those who have been trained by it.
>
> Hebrews 12:11

1. Students suspended from school must serve the entire term of the suspension as set by the administration. This includes students placed on in-school suspension. Leaving before the end of the prescribed time will result in the entire time needing to be re-served.

2. A student serving out-of-school suspension must write and submit a one page paper on what he / she did, why it was wrong, and what will be done to correct future problems of this nature.

3. All missed class work and assignments must be made up and ready to turn in at the time of reinstatement for credit to be given.

Behavioral probation and contract

Behavioral probation can occur at any time for major infractions. The behavioral probation will be initiated at the time of a parent conference with the principal. At this conference, a behavioral contract will be written with very clear consequences. It will be signed by all who are present (parent(s), principal, teacher). Failure to modify and improve his / her behavior in the next nine weeks could result in possible expulsion. A progress report will be issued three weeks following the initial conference and a review will occur after the ninth week.

Expulsion

> Why is there in the hand of a fool the purchase price of wisdom, Since he has no heart for it?
>
> Proverb 17:16

1. Expulsion may occur if repeated suspensions do not produce a change of student's behavior or attitude.
2. Expulsion is mandatory for the remainder of the school year for the following offenses that occur: involvement with drugs, alcohol, sexual immorality, use of weapons, or arson.
3. Students desiring to return to Salisbury Christian Elementary School the following year must receive the approval of the administration and the school advisory committee.

p. 11–16, expulsion in LC handbook
p. 40–48 in UC handbook

A. *Out of love*

The Scriptures exhort us to discipline our children because of our great love for them. Proverbs 3:12.

B. *24 / 7 / 365*

Students are accountable for their actions 24 / 7 / 365 on and off campus. A student may be asked to leave the school for encouraging inappropriate behavior in other students.

C. *Parent / school relationship*

The school reserves the right in every instance to discipline each case based on its unique and specific nature.

D. *Discipline guidelines*

1. Parent Communication (PC) is a written form communicating to the home information regarding a student's performance in school.
2. Behavioral Referral is a disciplinary action that attaches with it a Saturday school. Three PC's in a problem area such as tardiness to class will result in a Saturday school.

3. Suspension is a disciplinary action that results in the student's loss of privilege to attend classes for a determined amount of time. Suspensions run from 1–18 weeks.
4. Expulsion is a consequence resulting from behavior clearly contrary to the school culture and handbook at SCS. Expulsions run from 18–36 weeks.

E. Minor infractions

These will be handled through parent communication (PC) forms leading to the seven-step behavior referral format. (Refer to the behavior referral form on page 31.) The first commandment is devotion to God (Exodus 20:3). Minor infractions include the following types of behavior: disruptive, disrespectful, disobedient, unkind, tardy, being unprepared for class, or in dress code violation. When a student accumulates three PC's per teacher for the same problem or behavior, it then results in a behavior referral and suspension or Saturday school. It is the administration's decision as to which one the student will serve. On the fourth behavior referral, *a parent must attend each class with his or her child all day* within one week from the date of the infraction. Students will not be allowed to attend school until a parent spends the day at school. Students are expected to obey the clear teachings of God's Word (1 John 5:13).

F. Major infractions

Refer to behavior referral form on page 31. Immediately define the infractions as on or off campus. Administer correction as per on or off campus stated policy.

Major infractions include (but not limited to):

1. Drug and alcohol involvement (second and seventh commandments from Exodus 20:12–14).

2. Fighting, physical harassment or threats (sixth commandment from Exodus 20:13).

3. Excessive teasing or emotional harassment or gossip (sixth commandment from Exodus 20:13).

4. Extreme insubordination (fifth commandment from Exodus 20:12, in loco parentis).

5. Smoking or possession of tobacco (second and seventh commandments from Exodus 20:12–14).

6. Stealing / cheating / lying / slander (eighth through tenth commandments from Exodus 20:15–16).

7. Vandalism / graffiti (ninth commandment from Exodus 20:14).

8. Sexual misconduct (seventh commandment from Exodus 20:14).

9. Weapons of any kind (tenth commandment; Exodus 20:17).

10. Any illegal activity

G. *On campus*

On campus is defined as coming to or leaving from any school activity, the time spent in transit, and any time spent on the school campus proper or extended campus, for such events as sporting events, dances, field trips, retreat activities, etc.

H. *Off campus*

Off campus is defined simply as the time during which the student is neither going to nor coming from school, nor is involved on campus, nor an SCS sponsored activity.

I. *Zero tolerance policy*

We have a zero tolerance policy on fighting, sex, drugs,

alcohol, tobacco, stealing and weapons. It is our intention to protect our students from negative influences, intimidation and / or harm while simultaneously providing a clear stand for righteousness, love, help, and restoration for those students experimenting with or involved in behaviors contrary to their health, to Jesus Christ, and to the vision of SCS. The zero tolerance policy on fighting, sex, drugs, alcohol, tobacco, stealing, and weapons is as follows, as per Matthew 18:

1. Fighting, stealing, possessing weapons on campus will result in prompt expulsion. *We treat a threat as assault and any physical contact as battery.* Any unpermitted, harmful, or offensive touching is an automatic suspension.

2. Sex, drugs, alcohol, tobacco brought to school or involved in school will result in the student being expelled from school. This includes using any substance before or after school or at any school event and being affected by the substance *on campus.*

J. Suspension / expulsion policy

On and off campus restoration program includes:

First Offense

1. Up to eighteen week suspension. (Tuition will continue through the Independent Study Program.)
2. No involvement in any SCS activity.
3. Discipleship once a week (written confirmation) up to eighteen weeks through the Independent Study Program.
4. Attend weekly youth fellowship (written confirmation).
5. Twenty-five hours community service (written confirmation).
6. Twenty-five hours rehabilitation visits (written confirmation).

7. Up to eighteen weeks of Saturday school.
8. Reflection paper, five to ten pages.
9. Up to eighteen weeks of mandatory drug testing (if applicable).
10. Up to eighteen weeks probation.

Second Offense

1. Up to thirty-six weeks suspension. (Tuition will continue through the Independent Study Program).
2. One to twelve weeks of parent visits to school, all day, once a week (upon return).
3. No involvement in any SCS activity.
4. Discipleship once a week (written confirmation) eighteen to thirty-six weeks through the Independent Study Program.
5. Attend weekly youth fellowship (written confirmation).
6. Twenty-five hours community service (written confirmation).
7. Twenty-five hours rehabilitation visits (written confirmation).
8. Eighteen to thirty-six weeks of Saturday school.
9. Reflection Paper five to ten pages.
10. Eighteen to thirty-six weeks of mandatory drug testing (if applicable).
11. Eighteen to thirty-six weeks probation.

Third Offense

Student is expelled from school with no opportunity for readmission to Salisbury Christian School.

K. Cheating

A confirmed action of cheating will result in an immediate referral, a zero or *E* on the assignment, and Saturday school. Cheating is defined as:

1. Looking at another's test or quiz.
2. Using a cheat sheet.
3. Copying someone else's work including homework.
4. Complicity in cheating.
5. Any form of communication during testing.

L. Gossip, slander, lying policy

We believe gossip, slander, lying, cheating, and excessive teasing are as detrimental to the culture of Salisbury Christian School and our students as any outright excessive behavior. A student lying about a mistake will compound his or her discipline received. Therefore, our gossip / slander policy is as follows (as per Matthew 18):

1. First offense – Students work it out one-on-one. Behavior referral, suspension, or Saturday school.
2. Second offense – Public conference, behavior referral, one to eighteen weeks suspension / Saturday school.
3. Third offense – Student will be expelled.

M. Physical education non-suit policy

Please be advised that every time a student does not wear the complete PE uniform for PE or athletics, that student will receive a PC. Three PC's for non-suit will result in a referral and a Saturday school.

N. Pregnancy policy

We believe:

1. There is a need for all students to experience a personal relationship with Jesus Christ to mature as Christians.
2. Love, acceptance, and forgiveness should be the response to the student(s) that repent of their sin(s). (Luke 17:3–4)
3. Premarital and extramarital sexual intercourse is sin that carries severe long term consequences. (I Cor. 6:18–20)
4. Abortions terminate life and are not part of God's plan. Alternatives are available and must be considered when dealing with premarital pregnancy.
5. When an unmarried girl becomes pregnant, the father of the baby must carry an equal share of the responsibility with regard to the consequences of the couple's pregnancy.
6. Pregnancy and parenting should not be sufficient reason for dropping out of school and failing to graduate from high school.
7. All courses dealing with family life must emphasize the biblical principles of personal relationships, dating, marriage, sexual behavior, and the consequences of sexual immorality. Sexual behavior is defined as provocative, sensual, innuendo, dirty jokes; pornography; wet kissing; petting; intercourse; etc.
    a. Any on campus sexual behavior may result in an expulsion with no opportunity for re-admittance to SCS. Any discipline regarding off campus sexual behavior will be administered as per first, second, and third offense under zero tolerance policy. Because of the sensitive nature of a pregnancy and because the Bible clearly teaches *parents are primarily responsible for their child's upbringing, discipline, and restoration* (Proverbs 22:6, 13:24, 23:13–14, 19:18), any student who becomes

pregnant may apply for admission to the SCS Compassion and Discipleship Program. Those students must stay in that program for the full term of the pregnancy. If the pregnant student loses her child for any reason, the student will stay enrolled in the Compassion and Discipleship Program and must stay in that program for the duration of what would have been her pregnancy. The young man involved must also do the same. We believe firmly that God speaks to us through circumstances. Any major infractions, especially zero tolerance behavior, are a red flashing light for parents to renew their involvement in their child's life. It is our desire to simply be a supplement, not the primary solution, in the child's upbringing. God disciplines different people and circumstances differently (Romans 9:14–15). We are sensitive to God's leading in this area.

b. During the suspension of the expectant mother or father, or before any unwed mother or father may attend Salisbury Christian, the educational plan, counseling program, and terms of probation for the expectant / unwed mother and father will be determined on a case by case basis. This will be appropriate to the needs of each student involved and determined by the SCS administration with the assistance of an appointed counselor, the student's parents, and the student(s) involved.

c. Procedure: According to Salisbury Christian policies, sexual misconduct is considered a major infraction. For any major off campus infraction, students are given two options: (a) Participation in the Compassion and Discipleship Program for a minimum of nine weeks with academics through independent study at home, or (b) exit from the SCS school system. If the student decides to stay in the SCS System they must successfully complete all of the requirements of the Compassion and Discipleship Program. After a minimum of nine weeks, the Salisbury Christian Admissions Committee will evaluate the student. If the student is pregnant, the mother- and father-to-be will be recommended to the Independent Study Program at the time of evaluation. Both students (the boy and girl) will stay in the program for the full term of the pregnancy. During pregnancy and once a baby is born, we still desire to minister to the student / mother. The student / mother, once accepted to full-time status, may attend all SCS activities. For reasons stated in the next section, the baby must be kept at home with the family. Acceptance into the Independent Study Program is an ideal way for the students to continue their education at their own pace while dealing with the physical, spiritual, emotional and logistical issues that face them.

d. Reasons why the Independent Study Program is recommended:

   i) Physical: Teenage pregnancy is often high risk because the young girl is not physically developed yet. Her body is still changing, and with a baby developing inside of her the physical dangers are increased. Even if a teen has a fairly mild pregnancy, there may still be physical discomforts such as nausea and fatigue. Pregnancy requires special attention that cannot be given in a traditional school setting, such as maintaining a steady blood sugar, which requires a continual food / fluid intake.

   ii) Emotional: As an unmarried teenager, soon to be parent, the thoughts and emotions are not on the same plane as the other teenagers. Life will never be the same. Now the young couple must consider whether they are going to keep the baby or give it up for adoption. If they keep the baby, who will raise it? Where do the grandparents fit in?

iii) Spiritual: Both the mother and the father to-be will be faced with examination of their hearts before God. This time should be a time of forgiveness, healing, acceptance, and restoration. Based on Matthew 18:6, unmarried teenagers approaching parenthood can be, and have been, a stumbling block for other teens. For this reason we also ask that the baby be kept at home with the family.

iv) Final note: In the event a student who had used the self-referral process became pregnant after confessing, repenting and being restored, we want more than anything to love that student. To those who would suggest that we are unfair by requiring pregnant teens to leave school as a result of their condition, we return to our biblical foundation. God has ordained first parents, and then the church, to educate children. As a school we have limited resources in dealing with this complicated issue. We will support the child through Compassion and Discipleship. We will help design an academic program to insure the child's success towards graduation. Ultimately, however, it is the parents who must help their child navigate the turbulent waters of "Why me?" once the consequences of past behaviors begin to surface. "Pray without ceasing" (I Thess. 5:17).

O. Saturday school

Students receiving a behavior referral will be assigned to serve Saturday school from 7:00 a.m. to 12:00 noon. *Students will be required to serve their Saturday school on the Saturday within three weeks after the infraction date.* Tardiness to Saturday school will result in the student not being allowed to attend that day, and he / she will be reassigned to the following Saturday. If a student is absent from Saturday school, he / she will receive two additional days of Saturday school to be served the following two Saturdays. We are aware of the inconvenience this may cause, but request the utmost support as we all pray and work towards the same end. A signed doctor's excuse will allow the child to serve the next available Saturday school.

If a student is late or absent three times to Saturday school, he / she will be suspended *out of school for one week*. If a student has an assigned Saturday school day(s) which has not been served by the end of the year, that student will not receive grades. If the student is an eighth grader, he / she will not be allowed to participate in the promotion ceremony. If the student is a senior, he / she will not be allowed to participate in the graduation ceremony.

Please note: If more than one Saturday school is to be served, the parents may choose which Saturday to begin, but *all Saturday schools must be served in a consecutive, uninterrupted order.* Exceptions are made for school-recognized holidays. *All discipline is cumulative within the year.* We thank you for your support.

ACADEMIC AND BEHAVIOR REFERRAL

Salisbury Christian School

Love: Prov. 22:6, Prov. 23:13–14 **Discipline:** Heb. 12:1–13, Prov. 19:20

Student Name: _____ **Date** _____

Area of Concern

    Dishonest Tardy

    Disruptive Truant

    Defiant Unprepared

    Unkind Other

    (see below)

Comments

_____

_____

_____

_____

Teacher's Signature_____

Consequences:

First	One day suspension or Saturday school; letter and phone call to parents.
Second	Two days suspension or Saturday school; letter and phone call to parents.
Third	Three days suspension or Saturday school; letter sent to parents; phone call to parents.

*Fourth   Four days suspension or Saturday school; letter and phone call to parents; parent must attend school with student all day within one week of infraction.

*Fifth   Five days suspension or Saturday school; letter and phone call to parents; parent must attend school with student all day within one week of infraction.

*Sixth   Six days suspension or Saturday school; letter and phone call to parents; parent must attend school with student all day within one week of infraction; student is also placed on probation.

Seventh   Student is expelled.

*Please note: Parents *must* attend school all day with their child within one week of the infraction date for consequences four through six. Students will be withdrawn from school until parents visit the school.

This current Saturday school will be served on one of the next three Saturdays immediately following the date of this referral.

Choice one: date _____ Choice two: date _____ Choice three: date _____

Please contact the school office as soon as possible to reserve your child's suspension / Saturday school seat.

If more than one Saturday school is to be served, parents may choose which Saturday to begin, but all suspension MUST be served in consecutive, uninterrupted order. Exceptions are school-recognized holidays. All discipline is cumulative within the year. Thank you for your support.

Practical Arguments for Christian Curriculum

Curriculum is one of those areas with which you either love

to mess or with which you want nothing to do. A philosophy of curriculum is quite simple to develop. This statement of philosophy, like everything else, must first be funneled through the vision of the school. For example, if the vision of the school is "In All Things Christ Pre-eminent" (Col. 1:18), then the Christian school had better begin any curriculum review process with an eye toward the use of Christian texts exclusively.

Christian curriculum provides a cogent scope and sequence, that is, a menu or road map to what will be taught in each class each year. The ingredients to the menu or the city close-ups in the map are the curriculum guides. These curriculum guides are essentially detailed daily lesson plans. The lesson plans or curriculum guides explain the specifics going on in each class every day.

Christian schools must develop a ministry focus in the area of curriculum. The philosophy of curriculum will reflect the overall school vision. Prayer is fundamental to making a good decision. The pitfalls of picking a poor curriculum are many. Christian schools choosing secular curriculum without the leadership of the Lord can reap disastrous consequences.

Christian schools face several problems associated with selecting secular texts. The first problem is a worldview bias. By definition, the secular texts come from an existential, God-denying point of reference. The home-school movement, in large part, is a result of the insensitivity and outright hostility toward God in public schools. Christian schools using secular texts, without a specific call from God, are weak-kneed stepchildren of a wicked and horrifyingly manipulative stepparent.

Secular texts in a Christian school can undermine the authority of the teacher, school and adult influences in a child's life. How? you might ask. Consider the teacher that stops class and states, "Please turn from page 36 to page 41. We will not be covering that material in the book. The book says one thing and it is not true. I know I tell you to read the book for understanding, but parts of the book are in error. This is one such part." What happened here in that teacher's class?

The teacher just undermined her own authority by seeming to be inconsistent. Even though her explanation of why the material was unsuitable reflected certain integrity, the message was that she could pick and choose truth. Second, the publisher lost out simply because the teacher had to reject material as untrue. This also reflects on other literature. Notably, children may be inclined to adopt the secular view of relative truth as it relates to the Bible. What a tragic legacy of using secular curriculum.

In most Christian schools, teachers are often either very new to teaching or new to Christian ministry. This teacher background problem is one of the more serious concerns resulting from choosing a secular curriculum. The new Christian teacher is vulnerable to tremendous error in judgment as it pertains to teaching secular material in a Christian context. This problem could be alleviated somewhat with better training, but most Christian schools lack resources for adequate teacher training.

Christian schools should give a good hard look at an all-Christian curriculum. The Christian publishing industry is a multi-billion dollar enterprise. In all candor, Christian publishers can be narrow in their theological viewpoints. Likewise the material can be repetitious and, in some cases, offensive to other beliefs. In a few instances the material can be incorrect and the layout, teacher helps, and format stuffy and confining. The Christian school should do a thorough search for curriculum that fits God's call for its ministry.

Christian educators can only hope to foster results exhibited by the following story. This young man was raised on a solid Christian curriculum.

A college student was in a philosophy class where a class discussion regarding the existence of God was in progress. The professor had the following logic: "Has anyone in this class heard God?" Nobody spoke. "Has anyone in this class touched God?" Again nobody spoke. "Has anybody in this class seen God?" When nobody spoke for the third time, he simply stated, "Then there is no God."

The student did not like the sound of this at all, and asked for permission to speak. The professor granted it, and the student stood and asked the following questions of his classmates: "Has anyone in this class heard our professor's brain?" Silence. "Has anyone in this class touched our professor's brain?" Absolute silence. "Has anyone in this class seen our professor's brain?" When nobody in the class dared to speak, the student concluded, "Then, according to our professor's logic, it must be true that our professor has no brain!"

The student received an "A" in the class.

One last item to consider: In general, the written word is considered more influential than just about any other form of communication. This being the case, it would stand to reason that a Christian text sitting on a kitchen table could be used by God in a powerful manner. That Christian text could be used to evangelize a parent, grandparent, or other friend. Just a thought.

The following section, "Supporting Christian Curriculum," has been taken directly from a study on the matter commissioned by me to a group of parents. The bulk of the specific information was cobbled together by Mrs. Leigh Hughes. Her research has proved to be both biblical and practical. The findings require each of us to prayerfully consider what God is calling our schools to do.

Bible Verses and Quotes Supporting Christian Curriculum

> And be not conformed to this world, but be transformed by the renewing of your mind, that you may prove what is that good and acceptable and perfect will of God.
>
> Romans 12:2

> O Timothy! Guard what was committed to your trust, avoiding profane and idle babblings and contradictions (synthesis) of what is falsely called knowledge.
>
> 1Timothy 6:20

If religious books are not widely circulated among the masses in this country, I do not know what is going to become of us as a nation. If truth be not diffused, error will be; if God and His Word are not known and received, the Devil and his works will gain the ascendancy; if the evangelical volume does not reach every hamlet, the pages of a corrupt and licentious literature will; if the power of the gospel is not felt throughout the length and breadth of the land, anarchy and misrule, degradation and misery, corruption and darkness, will reign without mitigation or end.

Daniel Webster, 1823

I doubt whether we are sufficiently attentive to the importance of elementary texts.

C.S. Lewis
The Abolition of Man

Blessed is the man who walks not in the counsel of the ungodly, nor stands in the path of sinners, nor sits in the seat of the scornful; but his delight is in the law of the Lord, and in His law he meditates day and night. He shall be like a tree planted by the rivers of water, that brings forth its fruit in its season, whose leaf also shall not wither; and whatever he does shall prosper.

Psalm 1:1–3

Train up a child in the way he should go, and when he is old he will not depart from it.

Proverbs 22:6

Only take heed to yourself, and diligently keep yourself, lest you forget the things your eyes have seen, and lest they depart from your heart all the days of your life. And teach them to your children and your grandchildren."

Deuteronomy 4:9

The paramount philosophy of every false prophet is relativism.

R.C. Sproul

Do you know that friendship with the world is enmity with God? Whoever therefore wants to be a friend of the world makes himself an enemy of God.

James 4:4

Secularism is the new Idolatry. It takes the place of God.

Dr. J. Vernon Magee

Woe to those who call evil good, and good evil; who put darkness for light, and light for darkness; who put bitter for sweet, and sweet for bitter!

Isaiah 5:20

Whoever causes one of these little ones who believe in Me to sin, it would be better for him if a millstone were hung around his neck, and he were drowned in the depth of the sea.

Matthew 18:6

Do not enter the path of the wicked, and do not walk in the way of evil. Avoid it, do not travel on it; turn away from it and pass on.

Proverbs 4:14–15

Seek good and not evil, that you may live; so the Lord God of hosts will be with you, as you have spoken.

Amos 5:14

Beloved, do not imitate what is evil, but what is good. He who does good is of God, but he who does evil has not seen God.

3 John 11

Abhor what is evil. Cling to what is good.

Romans 12:9

Abstain from every form of evil.

1 Thessalonians 5:22

A Christian Worldview

A Classic Excellence in Christian education begins and ends

with the understanding that all our decisions are driven by our worldview. Cathy Duffy's discussion of "A Christian Foundation" (Chapter Five, *Christian Home Educator's Curriculum Manual 1997–98: Jr. / Sr. High*) helps us understand the vital importance of "building on a solid foundation" and "developing a Christian worldview" (33).

> *Worldview has come to mean "the type of philosophical framework through which we interpret all areas of life. Thus, a person might have a Secular Humanist worldview, a Marxist worldview, a biblical worldview, etc." (34)*

Because Duffy's analysis of the need for teaching a biblical Christian worldview is lucid and well thought out, I quote it extensively:

> *The Judeo-Christian worldview that prevailed in our country two centuries ago has been discarded or perverted so drastically that few even recognize what the worldview might be. Unfortunately, many Bible-believing Christians have become so confused by popular psychology, the media, government, and others with influence "the levers of power," as Don McIlvaney calls them, that their worldview suffers from distortion and inconsistency. A worldview should provide a coherent and consistent foundation for life. From that worldview we should be able to develop beliefs, positions, and attitudes about all areas of life (34–35).*

Could it be that the distortion and inconsistency seen in the worldview of many Christians might account for, at least in part, the results of a poll conducted by George Barna wherein he discovered that Christianity is having a "minimal influence on the thoughts, words, and deeds of people under the age of forty"? (*Religion Today,* as quoted by Ron Wells,

"Salt & Light," Feb 19, 1998) Barna's survey showed that across the spectrum of 100 indicators of attitudes, beliefs and behavior, "Christians are very similar to non-Christians in their everyday behavior" (Ibid.). *Religion Today* reports that Barna concluded from this data that "Christians are losing their impact despite the fact that 90 percent of Americans have a positive view of the Christian faith, and 84 percent believe themselves to be Christians" (Ibid.).

Christian schools must carefully and prayerfully consider the importance of inculcating our children with a solidly Christian worldview. We must ask ourselves what our maturing children will face when they have completed their high school education and,

- we must ask ourselves if we are equipping our children to, first of all, be able to stand firm in explaining their belief in Jesus Christ as Savior, and, secondly, to be able to bring the precepts of Christianity back into positions of influence in all those areas of life. Unless they understand how those areas of life are dominated by other belief systems, they obviously will not have any idea what changes are needed.

- we want them to be used by God. To equip them, an important part of their education is developing a biblical Christian worldview and, with that, teaching them how to examine all areas of life.

- at the same time, we also teach them how those holding other worldviews interpret these same areas. Unless they understand the presuppositions that form opinions, they are like gardeners trimming branches off a tree that is suffering from root disease. (Duffy, 35)

In Francis Schaeffer's *How Should We Then Live?* he suggests "People's presuppositions lay a grid for all they bring forth into the external world. Their presuppositions also provide the basis for their values and, therefore, the basis for their decisions" (*How Should We Then Live?* 19).

In one of his latest works, *The Patriot's Handbook*, Dr. George Grant provides an apt example of decision-making based on worldview values:

> *The transformation of American life from the colonial era to the national era did not so much hinge upon the prosecution of the Revolutionary War as it did the presupposition of a unique worldview. The worldview was inculcated in the colonies largely by the widespread Great Awakening—a dramatic revival of interest in, concern for, and practice of spiritual things. Sparked largely by the preaching of George Whitefield, an English evangelist, it was the single most significant cultural event leading up to the drive for independence.*
>
> Grant, The Patriot's Handbook, 69

Schaeffer elaborates:

> *Most people catch their presuppositions from their family and surrounding society the way a child catches measles. But people with more understanding realize that their presuppositions should be chosen after a careful consideration of which worldview is true. When all is done, when all the alternatives have been explored, not many men are in the room—that is, although worldviews have many variations, there are not many basic worldviews or basic presuppositions. These basic options will become obvious as we look at the flow of the past.*

As Christian school leaders, we must carefully weigh the impact of selecting curriculum for our schools. We are either raising up godly children with a strong Christian worldview or we are not. The notion that children, especially teens, can and will filter secular presuppositions through a biblical worldview with any consistency is spurious at best. *A Classic Excellence* requires our very best for our children as unto the Lord.

Tuition / Salary and Benefits

Tuition should cover operating expenses. That's it. That is the best philosophy of tuition I have ever heard. Christian schools notoriously fail to meet this most basic business fundamental. In the name of ministry, Christian schools tie themselves into knots trying to please everyone. Don't do this anymore.

Pray. Ask God for a vision for tuition that matches the vision of the ministry. God will bless you for sticking to your guns. Parents will look to the Christian school first as the church (handouts please), then as a bank (no interest loans for a year please), and finally as a phone company (look, I can't pay you this month but I'll pay you a little next month and the rest of my life till we get a little closer to caught up). Wrong. Please don't do this anymore.

The fallacy in this line of reasoning is the assumption that God will only work through the Christian school to help folks meet their needs. In some cases the Christian school acts as an enabler by continually allowing families to engage in poor budgeting habits, resulting in too much month left over after the money is spent. Consider God using a prayerful and compassionate Christian school, which has a sound policy on financial accountability, to help deliver people from the bondage of financial stress. Sometimes obstacles are opportunities disguised as problems.

In ancient times, a king had a boulder placed on a roadway. He hid and watched to see if anyone would remove the huge rock. Some of the king's wealthiest merchants and couriers came by and simply walked around it. Many loudly blamed the king for not keeping the roads clear, but none did anything about getting the big stone out of the way.

Then a peasant came along carrying a load of vegetables. On approaching the boulder, the peasant laid down his burden and tried to move the stone to the side of the road. After much pushing and straining, he finally succeeded. As the peasant picked up his load of vegetables, he noticed a purse lying in the road where the boulder had been. The purse contained many gold coins and a note from the king indicating that the gold was for the person who removed the boulder from the roadway. The peasant learned what many others never understood. Every obstacle presents an opportunity disguised as a problem. The Christian school financial policies and procedures should reflect clear purpose and afford much opportunity for God to work according to His purposes.

The Bible states that the worker is worthy of his wages. Christian schools are notorious for lousy pay, minimal benefits, and lackluster effort to change things. This is tragic. It is not biblical and it is an insult to Christ.

Let me explain. Salary and benefits in Christian school ministry are discussed as though the patient has cancer. Typically, the Christian school has a tuition structure that is entirely too low. Expenses are barely covered, if at all. Because the tuition is so low (presumably to allow more families to send their children), salaries and benefits are annually put on the back burner.

Christian schools focus on hiring is to employ mostly women teachers, (who usually have a husband making fairly good money), as well as retired male teachers. In many cases inexperienced pastors, church leaders or retired public school servants are placed in administration of the Christian school. Thankfully these servants honor God's call in their lives. Nonetheless, young teachers may cut their teeth in the Christian school, but generally leave after three to four years to support their family. Passion and continuity in the Christian school suffer greatly. They don't need to.

CHAPTER
eight

Cornerstones of Excellence

Let it be for the edification of the Church that you seek to excel.

1 Corinthians 14:12

THE POINT

I was a newly committed Christian. That is, I had finally decided to follow Jesus. I had accepted Jesus as Savior some five years previously. I was the seed that fell on the rocky soil, and was being choked by the cares of the world. I just couldn't seem to get into the groove of being a Christian. Things were different this time, though.

This time I was memorizing Scripture. I attended a mid-week Bible study, and church on Sunday nights (I couldn't quite get up in time for Sunday morning services). Interestingly, for the first time I was reading the Bible and understanding it, sort of. I started listening to Christian music, without throwing up. I also began praying to God.

The "Jesus thing" was starting to work for me. I was amazed!

Since I was now the seventh grade boys' basketball

coach I was, by definition, in a leadership position. I was well acquainted with the fundamentals of the game. I played competitively my whole life. I was especially zealous in keeping the boys well-drilled and conditioned. Though my intentions were good, I realized my focus was missing something.

The first clue that I was in way over my head came quickly. A tall, thin young man wearing wire glasses taught me much that first practice. I had just finished my opening pep talk. Big expectations, hard work, perseverance, and tenacity were going to be our hallmarks. I finished big, really big that day with seventeen seventh graders, each more concerned with how much time they would get to play. I asked if anyone had questions. My young, thin man had just one question: "Are we going to pray today in practice?"

Composing myself I mumbled "Great idea, Matthew. Will you pray for us?" Frankly, the thought had never crossed my mind. I was just like so many other Christians in Christian schools. I had Jesus in my heart but I didn't wear Jesus in my life. Little Matthew did what I had not yet learned to do. I had never prayed out loud to God. I learned two valuable lessons that day.

The first lesson I learned was that God had me at the school for what He wanted to do in my life, not just for what I brought to the party. God was doing a personal work in my life. This included my learning humility at the hands of a seventh grader. I learned that the best learning comes from doing. I learned that childlike faith is simple and powerful.

The second lesson I learned was that someone taught Matthew his boldness. Someone had modeled for him a personal, authentic, caring Jesus. The testimony of the lives that had been poured into Matthew's life over the years poured back upon me that day in practice. Call it the Law of

Eternal Giving. I understood, really understood, the practical importance of living a life of integrity in a consistent manner year after year. Lives for Christ are caught, not taught.

WIN

The cornerstone of excellence in the Christian school is Jesus. I have already discussed types of philosophies in the Christian school. It is imperative that, regardless of the school philosophy, the "Great Commission" is at the forefront of all that occurs in the school. Matthew 28:19 states: "Go therefore and make disciples of all the nations, baptizing them in the name of the Father, and of the Son and of the Holy Spirit."

Here are some biblical ideas for winning people to Christ in the Christian school. Weekly chapels should be a strong focus point. In preschool through fifth or sixth grade once a week is adequate. The key is having teachers trained to lead a child to Christ, and a faculty with a strong vision for in-the-classroom evangelism. Coursework, visiting speakers, and field trips are essential.

In the junior / senior high school, twice-a-week chapels are almost mandatory. Choices include a Monday and Friday lineup. This scenario helps with planning and avoids unnecessary tension between the faculty and the persons in charge of scheduling chapels. Another scenario is a Monday chapel to begin the week, or a Wednesday chapel to anchor the week. Additional chapels are then left to the movement of the Holy Spirit. This can become dicey if not everyone is aware of the vision as it pertains to winning children for Christ.

In the strong Christian school, everything the school puts out is an opportunity to win people to Christ. For example, all schedules, calendars, athletic and performing arts programs should always have the school vision prominently displayed.

Additionally, the school brochure should also have a tract-type format to lead people to Christ simply by having them read the school literature. Spring concerts, rummage sales, and fall festivals all afford the Christian school an opportunity to share the love of Jesus with the community. The well-run Christian school is unashamed of presenting God and the things of the Lord in a well-crafted, meaningful way. It is a matter of faithfulness.

Disciple

It is equally important to actively disciple the children *and* parents attending your Christian school. The Christian school represents individual lives. The faculty, staff, and administration must understand the principle that "a disciple is not above his teacher, nor a servant above his master" (Matthew 10:24). The best way to teach children about Jesus is to live for Him. Godliness is best caught, not taught.

Here are some biblical ideas for discipling children in the Christian school. An anointed adult should supervise chapels. Children in grades 3–12 should have increasing opportunities and responsibilities in planning and leading chapels. God does wonderful things through children who are properly supervised and open to His leading. When possible, worship should be student-led. Skits and drama components should be developed as soon as possible. Children love to act. Acting for God reinforces a child's faith. It also sends a very strong message to the student community in terms of the student-actor and the schools overall spiritual focus.

The superior Christian school should have a program in place that requires service to the community. This program should be completed within the context of each school year. It should be a graded part of a specific class, perhaps Bible or English. The administration of the program should be by the individual teacher and forwarded to the counseling or student affairs office for permanent record keeping. The administration should promote the program each semester. The Christian life is all about service. Examples include serving at Christian shelters, radio stations, newspapers, churches, etc.

To properly disciple a child, the Christian school must help the child learn how to effectively live his faith. In this context, every school function becomes an opportunity to train students in activating their faith. Consider student-led prayer at all sports and performing arts functions, student-led devotions at parent attended special occasions, and student-led testimonies at student-run functions like banquets, dances (if you have them), lock-ins, concerts, game nights, etc. In short, the Christian school must exercise faith to the degree that it is willing to allow God to lead children to minister—less professionally but more meaningfully—at all school sponsored events. Use your imagination.

Academic excellence is clearly the most significant aspect of discipleship. Christian schools with mediocre (or worse) academic performance do not have a viable testimony in the community. It is sad to see so many Christian schools simply forming a corporate shell with the best intentions only to stall on the fundamental reason for having a Christian school. Glorifying God is the number one focus area in any ministry. Christian schools must pursue academic excellence *and* a spiritual emphasis on Jesus. It can be done!

SEND

To send a child out from a Christian school with no awareness of how to share his faith is to send out a spiritual cripple. Christian schools must vigorously pursue opportunities that afford children the time to learn, practice, and apply their faith. The settings for activating their faith must be real. Acts 1:8 might be the calling card for a vibrant missions / outreach program in the Christian school: "But you will receive power when the Holy Spirit has come upon you; and you shall be witnesses to me in Jerusalem, and in all Judea and Samaria, and to the end of the earth."

Here are some biblical ideas for sending children out successfully into the world. First, for sixth, eighth, and twelfth grades, a class mission trip is ideal. This trip should be four to five nights for the younger students and well over a week for the older students. The trip should require faith in fundraising (discipleship), a clear, specific goal (for example to build one section of a house or to help clean up a section of a dump), and should require the complete support and participation of the parents (possible in-reach prior to the outreach). The school mission trip will undoubtedly become a class favorite.

In the fifth grade, seventh through eighth grades, and ninth through twelfth grades, respectively, the school should arrange a four to five day outdoor education or wilderness trip. The first purpose of the trip is to draw closer to Jesus. The next purpose should be to make better friends in Jesus. The third purpose should be to teach a variety of skills, depending on the locale. Examples of skills include ropes courses, teamwork in small groups, archery, life science, CPR, survival skills, endurance on hikes, compass use, animal husbandry and more. The wilderness trip really makes its mark in the evening around fires, with worship, God's Word, and openness to the Lord that only getting away to the outdoors can bring.

Grades three through twelve should be trained to go out and share their faith. Prayer, worship, devotions, and three-minute testimonies should be modeled for the child in the Christian school. The beach, mall, and shopping centers are all great places to bus small groups of students for a school day to apply their faith. This type of outreach may change your community. Students miss class time to go, but in the end it either reflects the vision of the school or it doesn't. If the vision includes sharing Jesus, go for it!

In Love

The Bible tells us they will know we are Christians by our love for one another. This is particularly important in Christian leadership. In Christian education (like much of life) administrators, board members, teachers, and parents have their own competing desires. The notion of dying to self is often lost in the pressures of child raising, financial constraints, and the like.

The focus in Christian schools must never move from Jesus to programs or policies. The simplicity of a personal love for Jesus must never be replaced by a choir performance, art contest, sporting event, or even academic excellence. Our love must never be diverted from seeking, serving, and sacrificing for the glory of God. We must be driven to pursue love over all else, passionate to pursue a raw Jesus. In a sense we need to have a childlike faith coupled with a paramour's love when we minister in the Christian school.

John Blanchard stood up from the bench, straightened his Army uniform, and studied the crowd of people making their way through Grand Central Station. He looked for the girl whose heart he knew, but whose face he didn't, the girl with the rose.

His interest in her had begun thirteen months before in a Florida library. Taking a book off the shelf he found himself intrigued, not with the words of the book, but with the notes penciled in the margin. The soft handwriting reflected a thoughtful soul and insightful mind. In the front of the book he discovered the previous owner's name: Miss Hollis Maynell.

In time and with effort he located her address. She lived in New York City. He wrote her a letter introducing himself and inviting her to correspond. The next day he was shipped overseas for service in World War II.

During the next thirteen months the two grew to know each other through the mail. Each letter was a seed falling on a fertile heart. A romance was budding. Blanchard requested a photograph, but she refused. She felt that if he really cared, it wouldn't matter what she looked like.

When the day finally came for him to return from Europe, they scheduled their first meeting at 7:00 p.m. at Grand Central Station in New York. "You'll recognize me," she wrote, "by the red rose I'll be wearing on my lapel." So at 7:00 p.m. he was in the station looking for a girl whose heart he loved, but whose face he had never seen. Here is what Mr. Blanchard experienced:

A young woman was coming toward him, her figure long and slim. Her blonde hair lay back in curls from her delicate ears; her eyes were blue as flowers. Her lips and chin had a gentle firmness, and in her pale green suit she was like springtime come alive. He started toward her, entirely forgetting to notice that she was not wearing a rose. As he moved, a small, provocative smile curved her lips.

"Going my way, sailor?" she murmured. Almost uncontrollably, he made one step closer to her, and then he saw Miss Hollis Maynell. She was standing almost directly behind the girl. A woman well past forty, she had graying hair tucked under a worn hat. She was more than plump, her thick-ankled feet thrust into low-heeled shoes. The girl in the green suit was walking away quickly. Mr. Blanchard felt as though he was split in two, so keen was his desire to follow her, and yet so deep was his longing for the woman whose spirit had truly companioned his own. And there she stood.

Her pale, plump face was gentle and sensible; her gray eyes had a warm and kindly twinkle. Mr. Blanchard did not hesitate. His fingers gripped the small worn blue leather copy of the book that was to identify him to her. This would not be love, but it would be something precious, something even better than love, a friendship for which he had been and must ever be grateful. Mr. Blanchard squared his shoulders, saluted and held out the book to the woman, even though while he spoke he felt choked by the bitterness of his disappointment.

"I'm Lieutenant John Blanchard, and you must be Miss Maynell. I am so glad to meet you. May I take you to dinner?" The woman's face broadened into a tolerant smile. "I don't know what this is about, son," she answered, "but the young lady in the green suit who just went by, she begged me to wear this rose on my coat. And she said if you were to ask me out to dinner, I should tell you that she is waiting for you in the big restaurant across the street. She said this was some kind of test!"

It's not difficult to understand and admire Miss Maynell's wisdom. The true nature of the heart is seen in its response to the unattractive. "Tell me whom you love," Houssaye wrote, "and I will tell you who you are."

TEAMWORK

The most noticeable ingredient missing from most Christian schools is teamwork. At this point you may be stopped cold in your reading. Good! If the concept of teamwork is foreign to you in the Christian school ministry then this section is for you. Read on.

Teamwork begins and ends with the Scriptures. First

Corinthians 12:4–20 gives clear instruction on the matter of teamwork:

> Now there are diversities of gifts, but the same Spirit.
>
> There are differences of ministries, but the same Lord.
>
> And there are diversities of activities, but it is the same God who works in them all. But the manifestation of the Spirit is given to each one for the profit of all: for to one is given the word of wisdom through the Spirit, to another the word of knowledge through the same Spirit, to another faith by the same Spirit, to another gifts of healings by the same Spirit, to another the working of miracles, to another prophecy, to another discerning of spirits, to another different kinds of tongues, to another the interpretation of tongues.
>
> But one and the same Spirit works all these things, distributing to each one individually as He wills.
>
> For as the body is one and has many members, but all the members of that one body, being many, are one body, so also is Christ.
>
> For by one Spirit we were all baptized into one body—whether Jews or Greeks, Whether slaves or free—and have all been made to drink into one Spirit.
>
> For in fact the body is not one member but many.
>
> If the foot should say, 'Because I am not an eye, I am not of the body,' is it therefore not of the body?
>
> If the whole body were an eye, where would be the hearing? If the whole were hearing, where would be the smelling?
>
> But now God has set the members, each one of them, in the body just as He pleased.
>
> And if they were all one member, where would the body be?
>
> But now indeed there are many members yet one body.

Teamwork begins in the Christian school at the front desk. The receptionist is perhaps the most important person on your team as it pertains to first impressions. The receptionist should be a servant: prayerful, discrete, a self-motivated person, and *not* a gossip. The receptionist should have an excellent relationship with everyone in contact with the school. Parents should trust her, teachers should be able to rely on her, the students should adore her, and the administration should barely notice her. A smooth reception area is effortless to watch, even in the midst of sick children, late mailings, early day dismissals and the like.

The excellent Christian school cross-trains all faculty and staff to properly answer the school phone. One suggestion is to answer the school phones, "Thank you for calling USA Christian school, this is Bob speaking, how may I serve you?" or "How may I help you?" Notice the emphasis on *serve*. Watch out for a school member who is reluctant to "go through all that just to answer the phone." Take ample time during the summer orientation to train everyone on when and how to answer the school phones properly. Remember that the phone is often the very first impression a family has of your school.

In addition to answering the phones with a classic greeting, it is also important to answer the phone promptly. Require your school phone to be picked up on the very first ring. Right away you will notice a newfound "sense of urgency." In schools that are really "humming" it becomes a fun game. Answering a phone on the first ring becomes a matter of school pride, especially if your school uses students to answer the phones from time to time.

Cross-training every faculty and staff member on a few critical areas of school procedures is essential to building a strong body working together, and not against one another in small factions. Phone etiquette, student and potential faculty application packs, and first aid emergency procedures are the bare minimum standards to be implemented school-wide in the classic Christian school. When (not *if*, but *when*) faculty or staff disagree with the idea of helping in clerical areas, it becomes time to pray.

Change, in general, is difficult. The godly leader will pray, communicate well in advance of any new changes, give folks time to pray and digest the new changes, and when the time is right, will implement the changes in love and with integrity and patience. However, some folks will still fight the changes. Understand it is here that true discipleship begins. The Christian school leader must discern if the issue is rebellion to authority or simply lack of understanding and fear. Teams are built on trust and hard work. Self-sacrifice must accompany any championship-level organization.

Another area of teambuilding should occur in the sharing of resources. Budgets are funny things. Once someone is told the have x dollars to spend in a given year, it is like prying a pearl from an oyster to make any changes later. A better approach is to ask faculty and staff for their needs for the coming year. The administration and department leaders prioritize the needs according to the vision for the coming year. Any monies left over (and there should be some) are disbursed through prayer as the Lord leads during the next year. People learn to *let go*. Likewise, when a parent wants to donate something to my class that I really don't need, I am thinking on behalf of the entire school and will look for ways to bless another teacher or department.

Pray—ask God for a vision for tuition that matches the vision of the ministry. God will bless you for sticking to your guns. Parents can tend to see the Christian school first as a church (handouts please), then as a bank (no interest loans for a year please), and finally as a phone company (Look, I can't pay you this month but I'll pay you a little next month and the rest of my life till we get a little closer to being caught up.) Wrong. Please don't do this anymore.

The fallacy in this line of reasoning is the assumption that God will only work through the Christian school to help folks meet their needs. In some cases the Christian school acts as an enabler by continually allowing families to engage in poor budgeting habits, which results in too much month left over after the money is spent. Consider God using a prayerful and compassionate Christian school, which has a sound policy on financial accountability, to help deliver people from the bondage of financial stress. Sometimes obstacles are opportunities disguised as problems.

In ancient times, a king had a boulder placed on a roadway. He hid and watched to see if anyone would remove the huge rock. Some of the king's wealthiest merchants and couriers came by and simply walked around it. Many loudly blamed the king for not keeping the roads clear, but none did anything about getting the big stone out of the way.

Then a peasant came along carrying a load of vegetables. On approaching the boulder, the peasant laid down his burden and tried to move the stone to the side of the road. After much pushing and straining, he finally succeeded. As the peasant picked up his load of vegetables, he noticed a purse lying in the road where the boulder had been. The purse contained many gold coins and a note from the king indicating that the gold was for the person who removed the boulder from the roadway. The peasant learned what many others never understood: Every obstacle presents an opportunity disguised as a problem. The Christian school financial policies and procedures should reflect a clear purpose and afford much opportunity for God to work according to His purposes.

The Bible states that the worker is worthy of his wages. Christian schools are notorious for lousy pay, minimal benefits, and lackluster effort to change things. This is tragic. It is not biblical, and it is an insult to Christ.

Let me explain. Salary and benefits in Christian school ministry are discussed as though the patient has cancer. Typically, the Christian school has a tuition structure that is entirely too low. Expenses are barely covered, if at all. Because the tuition is so low (presumably to allow more families to send their children), salaries and benefits are annually put on the back burner.

The Christian school develops a staff that is older, that consists mainly of women (who usually have a husband making fairly good money). Its administration usually consists of retired male teachers, inexperienced pastors, or church leaders in administration. Young teachers may cut their teeth in the Christian school, but generally leave after three to four years to support their family. Passion and continuity in the Christian school suffer greatly. They don't need to.

CHAPTER
nine

<u>*Classroom Excellence*</u>

You shall teach them diligently to your children.

Deuteronomy 6:7

Teaching is more than simply navigating children through a curriculum. It is personal. It is sacrificial. At its very core, teaching is going beyond all reasonable expectations. Teaching is the process of changing one life at a time. In Christian schools the fundamental change is a decision for Christ. But there is a more subtle change that occurs when ordinary teachers reach out beyond their wildest dreams or their elementary comfort zones. It is here on the edge that real, life-changing teaching occurs.

THE MASTER TEACHER

There is a story from many years ago of an elementary school teacher. Reading this from an e-mail someone had sent me, I immediately recognized this type of teacher from my own life. Perhaps you will too.

Her name was Mrs. Thompson. And as she stood in front of her fifth grade class on the very first day of school, she told the children a lie. Like most teachers, she looked at her students and said that she loved them all the same. But that was impossible, because there in the front row, slumped in his seat, was a little boy name Teddy Stoddard.

Mrs. Thompson had watched Teddy the year before and noticed that he didn't play well with the other children, that his clothes were messy, and that he constantly needed a bath. And Teddy could be unpleasant. It got to the point where Mrs. Thompson would actually take delight in marking his papers with a broad, red pen, making bold X's, and then putting a big "F" at the top of his papers. At the school where Mrs. Thompson taught, she was required to review each child's past records, and she put Teddy's off until last. However, when she reviewed his file, she was in for a surprise.

Teddy's first grade teacher wrote, "Teddy is a bright child with a ready laugh. He does his work neatly and has good manners ... he is a joy to be around." His second grade teacher wrote, "Teddy is an excellent student, well-liked by his classmates, but he is troubled because his mother has a terminal illness and life at home must be a struggle." His third grade teacher wrote, "His mother's death has been hard on him. He tries to do his best, but his father doesn't show much interest and his home life will soon affect him if some steps aren't taken." Teddy's fourth grade teacher wrote, "Teddy is withdrawn and doesn't show much interest in school. He doesn't have many friends and sometimes sleeps in class."

By now, Mrs. Thompson realized the problem and she was ashamed of herself. She felt even worse when her students brought her Christmas presents, wrapped in beautiful ribbons and bright paper, except for Teddy's. His present was clumsily wrapped in the heavy, brown paper that he got from a grocery bag. Mrs. Thompson took pains to open it in the middle of the other presents. Some of the children started to laugh when she found a rhinestone bracelet with some of the stones missing and a bottle that was one quarter full of perfume. But she stifled the children's laughter when she exclaimed how pretty the bracelet was, putting it on, and dabbing some of the perfume on her wrist. Teddy Stoddard stayed after school that day just long enough to say, "Mrs. Thompson, today you smelled just like my Mom used to." After the children left she cried for at least an hour. On that very day, she quit teaching reading, and writing, and arithmetic. Instead, she began to teach children.

Mrs. Thompson paid particular attention to Teddy. As she worked with him, his mind seemed to come alive. The more she encouraged him, the faster he responded. By the end of the year, Teddy had become one of the smartest children in the class and, despite her lie that she would love all the children the same, Teddy became one of her teacher's pets. A year later, she found a note under her door, from Teddy, telling her that she was still the best teacher he ever had in his whole life.

Six years went by before she got another note from Teddy. He then wrote that he had finished high school, third in his class, and she was still the best teacher he ever had in his whole life. Four years after that, she got another letter, saying that while things had been tough at times, he'd stayed in school, had stuck with it, and would soon graduate from college with the highest of honors. He assured Mrs. Thompson that she was still the best and favorite teacher he ever had in his whole life. Then four more years passed and yet another letter came. This time he explained that after he got his bachelor's degree, he decided to go a little further. The letter explained that she was still the best and favorite teacher he ever had. But now his name was a little longer. The letter was signed, Theodore F. Stoddard, MD.

The story doesn't end there. You see, there was yet another letter that spring. Teddy said he'd met this girl and was going to be married. He explained that his father had died a couple of years ago and he was wondering if Mrs. Thompson might agree to sit in the place at the wedding that was usually reserved for the mother of the groom. Of course, Mrs. Thompson did. And guess what? She wore that bracelet, the one with several rhinestones missing. And she made sure she was wearing the perfume that Teddy remembered his mother wearing on their last Christmas together. They hugged each other, and Dr. Stoddard whispered in Mrs. Thompson's ear, "Thank you, Mrs. Thompson, for believing in me. Thank you so much for making me feel important and showing me that I could make a difference."

Mrs. Thompson, with tears in her eyes, whispered back. She said, "Teddy, you have it all wrong. You were the one who taught me that I could make a difference. I didn't know how to teach until I met you."

THE MIXED MESSAGE

Christian classrooms must be so much more than a "safe place." Christian classrooms must be incubators of *REVOLUTION!* The world outside is a war zone. Every day in classrooms across the United States of America children are killing children. Adults prohibit the public display of the words, "Thou shalt not kill." In enacting a prohibition of the Bible in schools, public school leaders are inviting into schools the very hounds of hell. No wonder chaos, humanism, weapons, drugs, and now death are an everyday reality in classrooms across the country.

Here is a quote from Bill Bennett on the NBC Sunday talk show *Meet the Press* regarding the 1999 massacre at Columbine High School in Colorado:

> *If these kids were walking around that school in black trench coats, saying, "Heil Hitler," why didn't somebody pay attention? I guarantee you if Cassie Bernall (the young lady who, when she was asked, "Do you believe in God?" answered "yes," and then was blown away) ... if she and her friends had been walking through that school carrying Bibles and saying, "Hail the Prince of Peace, King of Kings," they would have been hauled into the principal's office.*

My dear friend, if we are not preaching Jesus in our classrooms, then we are setting up the next generation for an even greater calamity. The blood of the martyrs is already flowing in the streets, flowing in the halls of our schools and our Christian classrooms. It is time to be bold and unrelenting in inculcating our children in those things biblical. REVOLUTION! Live, breathe, preach, teach, model, be Jesus to your children. REVOLUTION!

Fun

In a very real sense, the next best piece of advice is to have fun. That's right, a classroom teacher cannot afford to take himself or herself too seriously. Remember, we are molding works in progress. Lighten up a little. Here is a cute story to illustrate the point.

On a special teachers' day, a kindergarten teacher was receiving gifts from her pupils. The florist's son handed her a gift. She shook it, held it overhead, and said, "I bet I know what it is, some flowers." "That's right" the boy replied, "but how did you know?" "Oh just a wild guess," she replied.

The next pupil was the candy store owner's daughter. The teacher held her gift overhead, shook it and said, "I bet I can guess what this is, a box of candy." "That's right, but how did you know?" asked the girl. "Oh just a wild guess," the teacher said.

The next gift was from the son of a liquor storeowner. The teacher held it overhead, but it was leaking. She touched a drop of the leakage with her finger and touched it to her tongue. "Is it wine?" She asked. "No" the boy replied, obviously delighted that he was the first student to at least temporarily defy the teacher's apparent insight. The teacher repeated the process, touching another drop of the leakage to her tongue. "Is it champagne?" she asked. "No," the clearly delighted boy answered. Once again the teacher tasted the leakage and finally said, "I give up, what is it?"

The boy enthusiastically replied, "It's a puppy!"

Like everything else, excellence in the classroom begins with a specific philosophy. In this chapter a clear philosophy of discipline and classroom excellence is outlined. Prior to explaining those philosophies, we need to take a moment and dispel one of the most tragic influences in the Christian school movement. That influence is Freud and his notion of self-esteem.

SELF-ESTEEM

Freud spent enormous time and energy attempting to explain man's nature within the context of man's worldly wisdom. His arguments, though logical, well written, and widely celebrated as truth within secular academia, were fundamentally flawed. Nevertheless, Christians, starved for a more intellectual approach to man's simple state of being, hungrily adopted Freud, his followers, and philosophies. Like the ancient Israelites who integrated idols into their culture against God's stern warning, Christian educators eagerly accepted as fact the flawed Freudian concepts of truth, man, and society.

It is time for Christian schools to dismiss, out-of-hand, Freud and the current secular philosophies that are so much a part of American secular *and* Christian education. Think for a moment, where are most Christian educators educated? Overwhelmingly, Christian teachers have degrees, credentials, and state certifications from secular colleges and universities. This in itself is problematic.

In fact, far too many Christian educators, from new teachers to administrators, simply do not know that they are products of a massive secularization of American education which began in earnest in the middle of the nineteenth century.

Freud, a notorious cocaine user and philanderer, set out to make man as the center of the behaviorist universe. Like Lucifer, Freud exalted his opinion above the truth of a triune God. The id, ego and superego, as well as the attendant notion of self-esteem, completely obscured the notion of man's sinful nature. Freud successfully altered the discussion from, "What is man's responsibility in his relationship with God?" to "What is the meaning of life for man autonomous from God?"

Freud introduced a three-part breakdown of man. Again, like Lucifer, Freud was misguided and manipulative. Recall that Satan asked Eve, "Did God really say this?" Casting a shadow of doubt in Eve's mind was all that was necessary for the next logical step: "Perhaps God didn't say this. Furthermore it may be that God didn't really mean what He did say anyway." This subtle yet powerful redirecting of truth was fatal for mankind in Eve's case. It is equally despotic as it pertains to the education of man, and has been growing increasingly destructive since the early twentieth century.

God made man in a three-part harmony. Freud understood this. Consider God's creative order and Freud's interpretation of it. God made man with a body. Freud defined it as the id. God made man with a soul in need of relationship with Him. Freud characterized this aspect of man as the ego. God provided man with a choice to receive His Spirit as a means of salvation, eternal fellowship, and wisdom to live a temporal life with meaning. Freud labeled this aspect of man's makeup the superego.

In addition to corrupting the nature of man made in God's image, Freud went further and replaced a relationship with God that, when consummated, produces fellowship, fullness, and peace with something called self-esteem. The fruit of self-esteem is man utterly alone, trying to sift through memories of an imperfect life spent separated from a loving God. It is the ultimate exercise in frustration, a type of hellish mental reincarnation. Self-esteem promoted man to godship. It also intensified man's loneliness, separation, and hopelessness.

American public schools are a philosophical descendant of Freud and the behaviorist influence of the nineteenth and twentieth centuries. Morally and spiritually, the public schools are a philosophical cesspool. How is it that

Christian schools are content to borrow from, and compare themselves to, a morally bankrupt, highly politicized, and deeply flawed secular methodology? Do Christian churches compare themselves to dictatorial cults? Christian schools must reframe the context of the question as it pertains to a philosophy of education. The notion of self-esteem by definition is worldly, some would argue that it is even demonic.

The superior Christian school recognizes that all of humanity has a sin problem. The school uses the term sin. In Christian schools we are sinners teaching sinners whose parents are sinners. Admit it, explain it, review it, and accept it. In this context we must teach this concept and others in love seasoned with grace. We need to understand that everyone will make poor choices. Everyone will feel bad at some point about who they are. Everyone will need the truth to get them through their time of trial.

Jesus said, "I am the way, the truth, the life" (John 14:6). Christian schools complicate matters when they bob and weave back and forth between secular methodologies and biblical truth. Instead of self-esteem, we need to talk about sin, grace, and Jesus' love. We need to rejoice. We have an answer to people's innate problems. We must do a better job of biblical discipleship. We need to do a much better job of loving one another.

It is a simple formula to live for God. Too often we choose to omit or ignore foundational truth for Christian living. It becomes expedient to simply "go with the flow." Christian educators become lazy when they borrow from the secular world. The compromise becomes the cornerstone of strife, and later of failure in the ministry. If Jesus is not the cornerstone of the school, then the ministry is in deep trouble. Too often, Christian leadership wonders why the ministry is stagnant and ineffectual. Graduates go off to abandon the faith, if they ever had any, faculty and staff leave because of a distinct lack of vision, and parents complain year in and year out about the same issues. Sadly, the Christian school becomes known as a safe place with regularly scheduled Bible studies. Pity.

It is the height of cowardice when we allow our children to whine and manipulate us into compromising situations. Too often children, sensing the ambiguity of the culture in which they live, use devilish reasoning to get parents and Christian schools to acquiesce to their self-focused desires. More Christian parents and administrators should heed the example of a pastor who communicated quite clearly to his children why compromise was less than desirable.

The pastor's children came to him and asked if they could watch an R-rated movie. They followed their question with a simultaneous barrage of justifications as to why this particular R-rated movie would be fine for them to watch. In the midst of the multiple appeals, the pastor remained silent. The basis of their argument was that this particular movie, while having some inappropriate language, didn't have much bad language. Charmed by the eloquence and tenacity of his children's logic, he simply responded that he would think about it and get back to them tomorrow.

In the morning the pastor was found in the kitchen dutifully preparing the weekend breakfast. His children bounded down the stairs to eagerly await his favorable judgment. So convincing had their arguments the day before been that they were assured of watching their cherished R-rated movie. Eventually the oldest child inquired, "Dad, have you decided to allow us to watch our movie?"

Quietly the pastor pulled out a tray of steamy, moist, chewy, chocolate brownies. They smelled as if the chocolate factory had moved right in. The children were astonished that their dad had even gone so far as to bake "movie munchies" for them. The pastor then paused and the whole world stopped. "Yes you may watch the R-rated movie if you will each eat these brownies as you watch the movie. I just need to alert you that the brownies, like your movie, have only a little something wrong with them. I added just a little dog do-do to your brownies, not much, just a little. Most of the brownies, like most of your movie, are wholesome and fine. Please dig in." His children never forgot that lesson. They also decided to ride go-carts that day instead of see a movie.

Christian schools must replace self-esteem with God-esteem. Instead of self on the throne and God outside ministering "on command," our self should be well under the lordship of God. Submission, obedience, and service are concepts that must be clearly communicated, taught and modeled in the Christian school. God is sovereign. Christian schools rise up and boldly proclaim the truth. We must live a measured life in a God-centered, God-esteemed manner.

Discipline

Academic excellence does not exist apart from a well-crafted and well-implemented school-wide discipline program. Discipline must always be firm, fair, and consistent. Corrective discipline sets out to treat the problem that has already occurred. Well over 90 percent of all Christian school discipline is corrective in nature. Corrective discipline must be administrated in love and seasoned with grace. Too much law pushes children away. Too much grace lets children drift away. The proper balance in discipline is critical.

Of course the very best type of discipline is preventative. Preventative discipline sets out to "nip the problem in the bud." Preventative discipline is most effective when it is prayerfully organized, and when the faculty and families are completely behind the administration. A few ways to promote school-wide awareness of problems before they occur in the high school are special chapels discussing drunk driving, sexually transmitted diseases, and the consequences of fighting and cheating.

In the middle school, special emphasis can be placed on kindness, cleanliness, cheating, lying and gossip. The middle school students very clearly need the rules spelled out and spelled out often. In fact, well trained middle school students cause much less trauma in high school if they have been properly trained and discipled in the middle school years. Too often middle school parents, administrators, and teachers develop the "middle school sigh" when discussing the students' behaviors and lack thereof. This is a tragedy and must stop!

In the elementary school, preventative discipline is easier to develop in the context of students generally having the same teacher for most of the day. Elementary students need moment by moment instruction before action is required of them. Likewise, elementary school teachers are wise to keep students active and engaged in learning right up through transitions into new subject matter. Teachers who give back to back instructions in grades 3 and above will be more successful with preventative discipline than those who do not. An example would be "clear your desks, take out your textbook and begin reading pages 22–23."

The very best lessons in life are learned the hard way. In Christian schools we would do well to understand the importance of having a sense of humor when dealing with our students. The following illustration is a superb example of corrective discipline turning into preventative discipline and becoming the ultimate "teachable moment."

This is for those who teach …

According to a radio report, a middle school in Oregon was faced with a unique problem. A number of girls were beginning to use lipstick and would put it on in the bathroom. That was fine, but after they put on their lipstick they would press their lips to the mirror, leaving dozens of little lip prints.

Finally the principal decided that something had to be done. She called all the girls to the bathroom and met them there with the maintenance man. She explained that all these lip prints were causing a major problem for the custodian, who had to clean the mirrors every night.

To demonstrate how difficult it was to clean the mirrors, she asked the maintenance man to clean one of the mirrors.

He took out a long-handled squeegee, dipped it into the toilet and then cleaned the mirror. Since then there have been no lip prints on the mirrors.

There are teachers, and there are Teachers…

USE THE SYSTEM

Pray! Use the system! It is that simple. Really, if every faculty and staff member simply used the discipline system within the school, then everything would run fine. Problems arise when people are inconsistent in using the system and make up their own rules. There are many fine examples of discipline in the classroom. The most important characteristic in the excellent Christian school is everyone understanding the discipline policy and everyone following the procedures for implementation. No lone rangers allowed!

Types of Classroom Discipline

Here is a very basic introduction to types of discipline styles found in classrooms across the country. The outline of this information can be found in the book *Making Children Mind without Losing Yours*, by Dr. Kevin Leman. Every administrator, teacher, and parent may benefit from the information that follows.

Discipline is a prerequisite to live an orderly and productive life. Discipline, correctly administered, allows us to see the character of God clearly. The Bible commands us to discipline our children and one another when necessary. Everyone involved in the life of a child must understand that discipline is a very important part of the child's training program. If this is not understood, discipline becomes very annoying to those that have the opportunity to build into the life of a child.

It is important to note that discipline is not punishment. Discipline is the development of a positive pattern of behavior. Discipline is the goal of punishment. Discipline is necessary for healthy decision-making throughout one's life.

The good disciplinarian is one who has control of the situation without injuring the learning process and environment of the child. The disciplinarian is also "solution conscious" rather than "problem conscious." Good discipline is consistent, decisive, and respectful, and is always based upon the reality of the situation. In Christian education we are sinners teaching sinners whose parents are sinners. Excellent Christian teachers recognize that every discipline situation is an opportunity to model Jesus, learn personally from Jesus, and maintain the high standards of the school while administrating the grace and love of Christ in a meaningful manner.

Authoritarian model

The authoritarian teacher robs children of their self-esteem (Christ-esteem). The authoritarian teacher makes all the decisions for the child. This type of disciplinarian uses rewards and punishments to control the child. This style is behaviorist in nature. The child is to respond in an anticipated manner or risk the disapproval of their teacher. Fear is a motivator here.

Rewards and punishments focus on the child and not on the behavior. Motivation for the child then comes from without and not from within. This type of discipline is often seen as "lording it over" the children. The authoritarian teacher sees him / herself as better than the child. This can lead to tremendous strife with parents and administration since this teacher is "never" wrong.

The authoritarian teacher runs his / her class with an iron hand. There is very little freedom to the child. This teacher is faithful to a fault in following the curriculum. In fact this teacher will be among the resentful when and if the school day changes and requires some flexibility on his / her part. Administrators need to understand that this person is neither excited nor supportive of anything that interferes with their plans. These teachers need to be encouraged with the phrase, "blessed are the flexible, for they shall not be broken."

This type of teacher fosters two types of behavior. First, students will model superior behavior in front of the teacher. This may also carry over before other forms of authority. The corollary to this type of teaching is that students will be rebellious when they are with other students. Unfortunately, students may also learn to view God as punitive, legalistic, and inflexible.

Consider for a moment an administrator, board member,

or parent with the authoritarian style of leading, oversight, or parenting. Christian schools are at the whim of differing styles of discipline. It is, therefore, the board and administration's job to clearly establish the school discipline philosophy statement. The administration then must enforce the policy with passion and consistency. There is nothing worse than a Christian school without a clear direction in the area of discipline.

I had the unfortunate opportunity to watch from afar the complete unraveling of a very fine Christian school system simply because the new administrator didn't understand the importance of casting a clear vision in the area of discipline. Compounding this oversight, the administrator felt it necessary to, at once, retain complete control over every discipline decision and cast blame on others when things understandably began to go sour.

In this particular instance, the administrator allowed friendships with parents, pressure or perceived pressure to please the church board, and personal insecurity to cloud any wisdom concerning the administration of discipline in their Christian high school. The result was a fractured trust within the faculty toward the administration. In short order, teachers stopped sending students to the office. Students sent to the office by teachers kept coming back to class with no administrative consequences and brought messages to other students that the administration was too busy and didn't really believe the teachers.

Likewise, parents began to doubt the integrity of the administration, since the lead administrator told each parent exactly what they wanted to hear. Eventually this duplicity caught up with the administrator. I believe we refer to it as gossip, slander, and lying when we discuss the same issues with children. Soon the teachers were walking on eggshells. A lack of support from the administration led to decline in student behavior, even though outwardly a strong focus on discipline was communicated home. Parents and teachers could no longer tell where they stood. People began making up their own rules. "And everyone did what was right in their own eyes."

The authoritarian administrator can be inflexible and dogmatic. Control at any cost is the hallmark of this type of administrator. The authoritarian board member will be critical and intrusive. The authoritarian parent will be legalistic and snobbish. In all three cases, nothing is ever done to the "standard." In the end the fruit of the Spirit can often be squeezed right out of the school. When that happens, the Christian school is in big trouble.

Permissive Model

The permissive teacher is almost the opposite of the authoritarian teacher. This teacher is the one who desires to be seen as "one of them." Their greatest desire is to be liked by the children. This style of discipline robs the child of their self-respect.

This style of discipline is confusing, especially for children in grades eight and below. The permissive teacher robs the child of self-respect by doing things for the child that he / she could do himself. This teacher is highly emotive. If someone in the class is not feeling well, the teacher may scrap the entire day's lesson to "minister" to that child. If confronted on being behind in the curriculum, this teacher may become very offended and hurt. Their concern then becomes the fact that the Christian school has now lost its way, and is on the verge of being apostate.

The permissive teacher makes assignments and classwork easy. Lessons are often redundant and unimaginative. Students are often given great authority in setting the tone and tempo for the class. This teacher is prone to being manipulated by clever students who trade the teacher's friendship for an unchallenging class.

The permissive teacher is so focused on pleasing his / her students, that learning suffers and discipline is non-existent. This teacher invites rebellion by promoting inconsistent behavior. The irony for this teacher is that the students, when alone, will discuss the fact he / she is "easy," a "pushover," or simply "clueless." This teacher is his / her own worst enemy. The tragedy is that the behavior promoted in their classroom spills over into other classes, and other teachers have to clean up the permissive teacher's sloppiness.

The permissive administrator is a study in futility. Unlike the authoritarian administrator who needs complete control, the permissive administrator craves complete acceptance. Underlying both motivations is the same issue, a dysfunctional focus. The permissive administrator is pleasant, kindly, and in many cases an excellent organizer. The problem arises when this administrator is faced with a difficult issue.

The permissive administrator is often the great compromiser. Victory for this person is in not upsetting either side. In always trying to always find the "middle ground," this administrator consistently frustrates everyone just a little. Usually the compromise is not quite offensive enough to merit full-scale war, but, in time, a series of bluffs and retreats by the administrator eats away at the integrity of the position and confidence is slowly lost in the position and the person. The permissive administrator, like the teacher, is more interested in acceptance and affirmation than in making a stand for what is right regardless of the outcome.

The permissive board member simply cannot understand how "we can expel this child for only smoking one cigarette." The permissive board member will question every discipline decision brought to the board in the context of "what will people think?" They will ask repeatedly, "Is this good for our school? Can we afford financially to let this family go? This family helped start this school, we can't do this to them!" Remember that we should not be fearful of doing what is right just because someone will react the wrong way.

The permissive board member will couch their questions in the context of the school's welfare. However, the underlying motive may be to keep the standards even since "my child may be next." Likewise, if people find out the board supported this position, and a permissive person is on the board, then he may be concerned about losing friends, influence and position. The permissive board member is more interested in harmony at any cost than principle and policy.

The permissive parent may not even show up to your meeting. This parent puts enormous authority into the hands of his child at a very early age. The child is seen in the eyes of the parent as an equal. The child's view of events in any circumstance is viewed as absolute truth. The school authorities are seen as impinging on the education and development of the permissive parent's child.

Permissive parents are often in the middle of horrendous sin and scandal in the lives of Christian school children. The reason is that these parents see nothing wrong with their children "experimenting" with life. Tragically, these parents may go off on a cruise for a week and not tell the school. They would arrange for an older sibling or relative to "check in" with their children while they are gone. When the keg party goes south and the school finds out, their response would be, "So what, it's not the school's business what our children do on weekends." They may never understand the temptation they placed before their children and others in, nor the responsibility they must shoulder in violating the integrity of the school's standards of conduct.

Authoritative / Responsible Model

This teacher builds self-respect and self-esteem (Christ-esteem). This teacher gives the child choices and formulates guidelines with him / her. This teacher has clearly established class rules. The students are keenly aware of the rules and the lines that should not be crossed. This teacher is in control of the process as well as the people.

The authoritative teacher provides students with decision-making opportunities within the context of orderly guidelines. This teacher develops consistent, loving discipline. There is no negotiating when an infraction occurs. Punishment or correction is swift and sure. Students are safe and secure within the standards established and the discipline executed in this teacher's classroom.

The authoritative teacher emphasizes encouragement that develops a motivation from within. This teacher trains children how to forgive. When the student is away from this teacher, there is a quiet reverence and heartfelt respect for the teacher. In some instances, students speak about having this type of teacher as if they were wearing a badge of honor.

The authoritative teacher holds students accountable. This teacher lets reality be the teacher. Students are rewarded for meeting standards and suffer consequences for falling short. This teacher disciplines by way of action, not by way of anger. The idea that "anger assassinates relationships" is not lost on this teacher.

The authoritative administrator is someone who is viewed by virtually all in the Christian school family as prayerful, consistent, truthful, and loving. People do not discuss the authoritative administrator in terms of their latest decision. This type of administrator demonstrates daily that the wisdom of God is his / her benchmark. Neither swayed by man nor by position, this administrator develops standards of behavior in conjunction with the board, teachers, and parents. Then the administration of policies and procedures is consistent, swift, and sure.

The authoritative administrator is people oriented. This person is mindful of the fact that Jesus touched people. This administrator is inclined to suffer much for the cause of Christ. In touching people, this administrator places him / herself directly on the firing line. To be vulnerable is to be open to sniper fire. The authoritative administrator engenders great trust and respect from teachers, parents, board members and students alike. The authoritative administrator runs a school without fear or manipulation where the gifts of the Holy Spirit are evident and in effect.

The authoritative board member is prayerful. This person understands the boundaries of authority in the operation of the school. This board member will serve enthusiastically and never cross the line into operations. This person is a protector of the flame of vision that God has given the school. This person supports the administration publicly through thick and thin. When appropriate, this board member will support change.

The authoritative board member encourages the administration. The authoritative board member consistently promotes the Matthew 18 principle in all discussions regarding the school, especially at summer picnics and Christmas parties. The authoritative board member asks hard questions of the administration at board or committee meetings, follows up those questions appropriately, and yet always speaks with a spirit of genuine concern and love.

The authoritative parent understands his child probably "did do it." This parent is not easily offended. This parent asks probing questions to seek out truth. This parent makes it clear that they are in full support of the school and its administration.

The authoritative parent is easily entreated. This parent is involved in his / her child's life, but is neither consumed by nor absent from the child's life. This parent desires high standards in a balanced and loving environment. Without hesitation, the authoritative Christian parent desires Jesus to first and foremost in all the school does for their child.

Authority and Discipline

One question everyone in Christian education needs to consider is, "Does a person need more authority or does he / she need to improve the authority they already have?" The following components determine a person's authority. When any of these areas are flawed it compromises that person's effectiveness in administering or leading their classroom or Christian school.

Position is the least important factor in establishing and implementing authority. Saul had position but young David had authority. It took Saul years of mental fatigue, spiritual breakdown; attempted murder, humiliation, and the like before God elevated David to the position of king. In the meantime, how many people thought to themselves that Saul is mad? How many times did David go before the Lord and share his justifiable hurt?

Christian schools can learn a valuable lesson here. Authority is God-breathed. Prayer is the most effective means to change authority. Christians need to stop complaining and start praying. Those in authority whose sole claim to such is their position are in a dangerous place indeed. It is here that much incompetence in the Christian school occurs.

Competence is important in the elevation of one's

authority. It is more important than position and often requires time to develop. Christian schools are notorious for raising up leaders only to shortchange their authority by underfunding and understaffing the Christian school. A cogent plan to develop the authorities in charge of the Christian school is essential to the school's future health. Graduate school, seminars attended by board and administration, as well as meaningful leadership retreats are a must for any successful Christian school.

Personality is a strong natural indicator of potential authority. Personality, more than any natural talent, reflects God's gifting of a person. The administrator / leader who has the personality to assume authority will be naturally disposed to carrying out the responsibilities inherent in the use of authority. The spiritual gifts of leadership and administration fall most easily into the personality of the administering authority.

Character is developed. All authority is given by God and delegated to man for God's purposes here on earth. God will inevitably give the person with a strong character much responsibility on earth. Position, character, and personality are fundamental to determining a person's authority.[8]

The things that frustrate students when it comes to authority are adults being fleshly about their position of authority. Some examples of student frustration include the attitude among adults that "I am the boss." Double standards are always a negative influence. In one Christian school the school rule was that students could have no drinks other than water, and there was to be no eating in classrooms. One teacher took it upon herself to skirt the rules by drinking soda from a covered water bottle. When asked by a fellow teacher and department leader, she lied and said it was water. Her students knew she lied. Her example was deceitful, and her authority was undermined.

Authority figures that are always judgmental are tiresome and frustrating to deal with. A lack of consistency is always a problem in any authority position. Lack of consistency erodes the confidence of people in both the institution and the person in authority. The final frustration for students deals with those in authority not taking the time to listen to students' concerns. Jesus listened to people; those in Christian ministry should also do the same.

Basic components of effective discipline include the following characteristics: love, instruction, reinforcement, and correction. This list is far from complete. First and foremost, effective discipline requires a genuine love for people. Bathing every aspect of discipline in prayer is a strong beginning when handling all discipline. Love is a choice. Effective discipline requires a conscious choice by those in authority to love those under authority, unconditionally.

Proper instruction is a key element to promoting effective discipline. The finest Christian schools require parents and students to read their handbooks in the summer. Students and parents then sign and return a commitment to support the school and to follow its stated policies. This happens at the end of the first week of school. Next, the school spends some classtime once a semester to read every page in the handbook so that all faculty, staff, and students are familiar with the school policies, procedures, and consequences. This is an example of proper instruction.

Reinforcement is critical to increasing awareness of and implementation of sound policies for discipline. Classroom teachers reward students by being first in line with good behavior. Christian schools reinforce school-wide standards by using public forums to highlight student achievement, awards banquets to promote academic excellence, and special chapels to highlight superior behavior and attendance. The possibilities for reinforcement are endless. One Christian school administrator would visit every classroom once a week and pick one student in each class to bless with a candy bar. His students and teachers understood what he was focusing on.

The idea of correction is highly overrated. Correction, or consequence, is nothing more or less than the administration or authorities simply doing what they said they would do. Students and families make poor choices. Faculty and staff may make poor choices too. When this happens, the authorities must look to already formulated policies and procedures and simply execute the consequences of those policies and procedures. There is entirely too much time spent during a crisis or time of discipline discussing the merits of the punishment vis-à-vis past instances, current policy, etc. Those in authority would do well to simply carry out the consequences and move on. Do what you said you would do.

In the interest of clarity the following should be noted: the time to discuss policy and procedure revision is not during a crisis. Typically February, March, and April are the months to brainstorm with students, parents, faculty, administration, and the board. Once this system is in place, people will understand that even though they don't agree with a particular aspect of the school's operation, they will be given a chance annually to change things in an orderly and prayerful manner.

TWO SIMPLE CLASSROOM RULES

The following two classroom rules are applicable in any classroom grades K through twelve.

1. No communicating without permission
2. No getting out of your seat without permission

Consider the ramifications of each rule. These two rules cover everything else. Communicating includes notes, hand and facial gestures, words, frowns, grunts, and any other form of communication. Not being able to leave their seat takes away mobility. These two rules should cover it for any teacher in any class. Try them!

CHAPTER
ten

Operational Excellence

This Book of the Law shall not depart from your mouth, but you shall meditate in it day and night, that you may observe to do according to all that is written in it. For then you will make your way prosperous, and then you will have good success.

Joshua 1:8

ADMISSIONS

Admissions standards in Christian schools are derived from one of two fundamental philosophies. The first comes from Reformed Covenant Theology. It presupposes that the children attending the school are coming from strong Christian homes, and are Christian themselves. Churches with a conservative or strong Calvinist predisposition typically adhere to this view. Evangelism is done in the home. The school is designed primarily as a tool for discipleship to strengthen what is valued in the home.

The second philosophy is more evangelical. It states that schools should view children as a modified mission field. Evangelism in chapels, through sports, the arts, and classroom instruction is viewed as perfectly normal. This philosophy understands that some parents may not be saved, even though they say they are. Likewise many children may not yet be saved.

These two philosophies are rarely static. Strong fundamental reformed schools become stale, lukewarm, and uninspired in living their faith day to day. The more evangelical approach can spawn periods of rebellion and possibly confusion if proper care is not given to the admission of non-saved children and families. In some cases, a small handful of rebellious children can negatively affect an entire school. A little leavening leavens the whole lump.

Admission is the gateway to the heart of the school. It is important that everyone in the Christian school understands the vision of the ministry. It is equally important that everyone grasps the fundamental truth underlying all of Christian education. In Christian education we are sinners teaching sinners whose parents are sinners. Saved or not, we all have a sinning nature. It is the height of presumption to believe we will educate an entire school of holy children unto the Lord.

Let's be frank. Children make bad choices. Sometimes these choices are willful, sometimes they are not. The admissions procedure is established to identify those folks the Lord has called to the Christian school. The first and most important question to be asked then is, "has God called this child and family to the school?" Be careful when you ask this question. The Bible says, "for God's ways are not our way, nor His thoughts our thoughts" (Isaiah 55:8). Remember also "that man looks on the outward appearance, God looks at the heart" (I Sam 16:7). In any event, it is a privilege and not a right to attend your Christian school. Proceed in the process accordingly.

One year as a high school principal I accepted a homeless boy with tattoos, dreadlocks, and a pierced nose. I also accepted a girl who had a B+ average in school, was a cheerleader, and class president. She transferred from another Christian school. Her parents were godly people. Finally, I accepted a young black boy on financial aid from a very poor section of town. He had an alcoholic father and a mother who worked two jobs.

In the course of the time the students were with us, I witnessed something very interesting. The boy with tattoos and dreads became on fire for Jesus. He wrote music, formed a band, signed with a label, produced a Christian Rap CD, and toured the country. He was a vocal, outspoken supporter of Christ on campus. He was a leader, in a grunge sort of way. He learned to study and did well academically. He went on to become a well-rounded young man, and a doting father. That is, after we expelled him for getting a young lady pregnant in his senior year!

The B+ class president likewise did well in school, for two years. Then the wheels fell off the wagon. In short order, she began to frequent rave parties. She encouraged other students to join her. Since she was so popular, many other students chose to fall into sin. Though she was an asset to the school, she also didn't graduate. She was expelled due to her negative influence on other children, which undermined the philosophy of the school.

The young black man had a difficult time adjusting to our school. He had very low test scores and barely knew how to read. His self-esteem (or Christ-esteem) was also terribly low as well. It was "day to day" with him for a number of years. Each year he threatened to quit and return to his neighborhood school. Somehow at the end of six years he graduated. During his time at the school a quiet, strong faith had taken hold.

The moral behind the illustrations is clear. Only God knows the hearts of man. We look at nice attire, a good family, and strong grades, and we automatically assume that we are admitting a godly child. Conversely, we may fear the unkempt, low scoring child of a single parent, because they seem not to fit into our optimum school profile. Remember that the main question to answer is whether God called the child and family to the school. Do not get caught up with appearances. Let God be God. Everything else will take care of itself.

Here are some practical ideas for increasing enrollment through admissions in your Christian school; I refer to these as the "nifty fifty."

1. Pray for God to bring whomever He wishes to your school.
2. Develop your admissions philosophy, and communicate it clearly to everyone in your school family.
3. Track all inquiries in a database, and periodically mail to interested families updates on your school.
4. Train teachers to write, call, and meet with parents of children in their classes to encourage continued relationship with your school.
5. Hold Shadow Days in February. Students in grades 3 through 12 are encouraged to invite a friend to visit school, to "shadow" them for a day. Schedule a chapel, lunchtime or recess time competitions, or other special surprises throughout the day. Schedule third through fifth grades on a Tuesday, sixth through eighth grades on a Wednesday, and ninth through twelfth grades on a Thursday. Word of mouth (students asking

students) will bring a powerful witness to your school's admissions program. Invite students from every school (public or private) in your area.

6. Host a new parent orientation meeting the week before Shadow Days. Invite all potential new families to this meeting. Explain what their child may expect, answer questions, and hand out admissions information. School cheerleaders in uniforms, the student body president, and student testimonies for Christ and for the school should all be highlighted.

7. Host a Pastor Appreciation Day in March. Invite all pastors in your community to a special day of music, drama, arts, eats and Jesus. It's a great way to showcase your school while blessing pastors as they travel part of a day with students who attend their church.

8. Send school information packets to realtors, Welcome Wagon organizations, chambers of commerce, etc.

9. Write and release weekly press releases in local papers, radio, and television. Pay particular attention to free exposures. These include calling in sports scores, touting academic achievements, extracurricular excellence, high SAT scores, and student-led efforts in community forums.

10. Consider the board and administration meeting in small home fellowships once a year in April to recast the school vision, pray, and fellowship with families. It is generally five times as expensive to recruit a new family as it is to retain an existing one.

11. Offer discounts to families that refer students who are accepted to enroll in your school.

12. Fight to retain wavering families if you sense that the Lord would have them stay. Offer scholarships or financial aid. The key is to try not to have any empty seats, and to keep your best students.

13. Set up mailing lists for grandparents, alumni, and current families. Prayerfully prepare a tasteful mailing at least twice a year, and mail it to everyone on your lists. Include as many people in your school family as possible.
14. Conduct exit interviews with all families who leave your school. Look for patterns that need correcting.
15. Establish, develop, and execute a prayerful and well thought out plan for academic and extracurricular excellence in your school. Excellence draws in quality students, families, and resources.
16. Mail thank you notes to everyone who helps with anything in the school.
17. Mail birthday cards to every student, faculty, and staff member. You can have an amazing impact remembering someone's birthday! Remember to be proactive.
18. Encourage staff members to pursue presentations at local, regional and national functions. Rotary, VFW, Christian seminars, and more are all fine places to promote your school by simply being active in the community.
19. A publicity team from the board or PTF should help by putting up posters and handing out flyers in the community. Drama productions, re-enrollment dates, concerts, and other school activities should be regularly advertised by the publicity team.
20. Develop a student store. Sell school hats, shirts, jackets, bags, bumper stickers, book covers, etc. This will also elevate school pride.
21. Emphasize missions in your community. Actively seek out opportunities to serve in your community. Homeless shelters, adult care facilities, and Habitat for Humanity are some service ideas. School choir, drama participants, cheerleaders, art club members and others

would benefit greatly from this type of experience.

22. Contact local print, TV, and radio organizations and ask to be interviewed.

23. Develop your school's own Web page. Use this to expand the reach of your school's vision.

24. Communicate with your database via e-mail as often as great news occurs in your school.

25. Open up your school to be used by other ministries and local organizations. This will build good will and provide another type of exposure for your school.

26. Be flexible! In smaller Christian schools, not everything a child needs can be offered. Do not let a child transfer for this reason. Work hard to accommodate the child's needs via the public school system, independent works, the state community or university system, etc. Be creative!

27. Implement an "open door" policy for students needing to be expelled. Once expelled, a student should have the chance to return and try again. This merciful approach is pleasing to God and will be blessed.

28. Promote the best of your school in a school calendar, publication, video, etc. Give this to local businesses, ministries, schools, etc. To fund the project include the costs in the budget, use advertising monies, or use Annual Fund drive monies.

29. Give extra yearbooks to doctors, dentists, and lawyers around town for their waiting areas.

30. Use well crafted signage to advertise your school around your campus.

31. Use your chapel program to reach out and minister in local preschools, elementary schools, and the like. Use your students' gifts to reach out to Boy Scouts, Girl Scouts, YMCA groups etc. The possibilities are endless.

32. Include school brochures and tracts in all outgoing mail, including bills.

33. Have a scheduled "Open House" advertised throughout the community. Schedule at least one "Open House" in August, September, January, and February.

34. Make sure your school is properly listed in the phone book, Chamber of Commerce magazine, Welcome Wagon, literature on the Internet, and anywhere else the school is listed.

35. Invite community leaders to speak at your school. Encourage the mayor, judges, senators, and others to use your school as an opportunity to meet and influence young people.

36. Send information on your school to every child born in your community. This will impact your school in the next five years.

37. Encourage the school PTF to enthusiastically support and promote the school vision in the community. PTF recruitment via word of mouth will be among the most powerful tools for improving admissions at your school.

38. Promote high standards in your school. Do what you said you would do. Do the right thing because it is right to do the right thing. Never be a man pleaser. Relax, and always trust God!

39. Promote school-wide bonding events such as bonfires, alumni games, homecomings, retreats, concerts, speakers, etc.

40. Implement a parent-student evaluation form to be filled out and returned to the headmaster no later than May 15th. Use the information and suggestions to improve your school.

41. Purchase the finest uniforms for your teams to wear. Sometimes a school's athletic teams are the only

memorable representatives the community sees.

42. Compete in every local, regional, and state competition for which your school can organize a team. The more exposure your school gets the better your students perform and the stronger your school's name recognition becomes.

43. Enter your school in local parades and festivities. Consider being a sponsor for another school's fundraiser. Remember: exposure, exposure, and exposure.

44. Promote your school's distinctive qualities such as tutoring programs, student-teacher ratios, championship teams, SAT scores, and college placement.

45. Expand your school's program offerings to include such groups as learning disabled students, international students, ESL students, and home-schooling students.

46. Answer the phone on the first ring. This includes the receptionist, secretaries, principals, and headmaster. Everyone should treat the phone as the lifeline to the ministry.

47. Have registration materials handy at the front desk of each campus. Everyone in the office should be cross-trained to handle any request for information. Never, ever turn a request away because of lack of information.

48. Consider a money back guarantee.

49. Establish high standards of behavior, academics, extracurricular programs and operations. Inspect what you expect. Execute what you implement.

50. Love the children, and love one another. Love the Lord with all your heart. He will take care of the rest.

Physical Plant

Christian schools are notorious for using second-rate facilities, church basements, inadequate athletic fields, and worse. Stop! It is time for the Christian community to quit whining about how difficult it is to … you fill in the blank. We serve the one, true, living God. Yet Christian schools are, in so many cases, stuck in the mode of school start ups circa 1950. Why?

We have already covered the philosophy of tuition, salary, and benefits. The same fundamentals hold true in the area of physical plant. Our goals should be prayerfully developed. If God were calling you to start and run a first-rate Christian school, then that should include a superior physical plant. More often than not, though, something doesn't translate from start-up to mature excellence in many Christian schools. Why is that?

The reasons for inadequate physical plant quality in Christian schools are threefold. First, the school leadership has a lack of clear vision. Without a clear vision, the ministry will begin to stagnate and lose momentum. Momentum is the single most important intangible asset a school has. Without it, mediocrity sets in. The best people move on, and the school becomes a glorified Sunday school or worse.

Second, the school leadership has a crisis of belief. The Bible is clear that "without faith it is impossible to please God" (Hebrews 11:6). Henry Blackaby speaks of the need, at some point, to "live by faith." The lack of faith is symptomatic of a lack of vision. Lack of faith is the final spiritual straw, so to speak. The Bible is clear, "without faith it is impossible to please God." At this point the Christian school is in the process of dying.

A third reason for poor and inadequate facilities is the

Operational Excellence 215

flesh. People with agendas are the death of any ministry. Christian schools literally stagnate and atrophy right before everyone's eyes when the leadership does not present a clear picture of what the Lord wants. Leadership without a vision is truly the blind leading the blind. Nature abhors a vacuum. Where there is indecision, infighting, manipulation, and politicking, the Spirit of the Lord is surely to be grieved.

Here is a parable from Horizon Christian Fellowship's discipleship training program manual that speaks to the importance of vision:

For months, the Fisher's Society had been wracked with dissention. They had built a new meeting hall which they had called their Aquarium, and had even called a world renowned Fisherman's Manual scholar to lecture them on the art of fishing. But still no fish were caught.

Several times each week they would gather in their ornate Aquarium Hall, recite portions of the Fisherman's Manual, and then listen to their scholar exposit the intricacies and mysteries of the manual. The meeting would usually end with the scholar dramatically casting his net into the large tank in the center of the hall and the members rushing excitedly to its edges to see if any fish would bite.

None ever did, of course, since there were no fish in the tank. Which brings up the reason for the controversy. Why? The temperature of the tank was carefully regulated to be just right for ocean perch. Indeed, oceanography experts had been consulted to make the environment of the tank nearly indistinguishable form the ocean. But still no fish.

Some blamed it on poor attendance at the society's meetings. Others were convinced that specialization was the answer; perhaps several smaller tanks geared especially for different age groups would work better. There was even division over which was more important: casting, or providing optimum tank conditions? Eventually a solution was reached.

A few members of the society were commissioned to become professional fishermen and were sent to live a few blocks away on the edge of the sea and do nothing but catch fish. It was a lonely existence because most other members of the society were terrified of the ocean. So the professionals would send back pictures of themselves holding some of their catches and letters describing the joys and tribulations of real live fishing. And periodically they would return to Aquarium Hall to show slides. After such meetings, people of the society would return to their homes, thankful that their hall had not been built in vain.

Too often Christian schools, like churches, begin to settle down. When this happens and the true heart of the Lord is lost, the school may begin to travel a course "two degrees off." In sailing, two degrees off is the difference between arriving in San Francisco or Panama if beginning a voyage from Tahiti. The notion of missing the mark is lost in much of Christian ministry. The reality is that we can and do miss the blessing of God because of sloppy or inept planning. Likewise, if we lose our passion for the vision Christ has given us our compromise becomes, in effect, a type of surrender into an oblivion of mediocrity.

Some Christian schools are overgrown with the mold of apathy and briars of fear. This can be like weeding a rose garden overgrown for the last ten years. These schools would just as soon tell you "we are already all God wants us to be." This may be true. It may also be what once was true. Changing schools like this is often impossible. It can be hard work. It can be painful and time consuming. I experienced that in my first tenure as a Christian school headmaster.

The school God called me to was thirty-three years old. The school went from pre-school through the twelfth grade.

Operational Excellence 217

My first year at the school was also the first graduating class of twelfth graders. In the preceding five to six years the school had gone through some turmoil, to be sure. I only realized this upon my arrival.

First, the preceding headmaster had grown the school magnificently, but had burned out. For the next two years, the school board had "run" the school without a lead administrator. The two schools' principals were both retired public school administrators, yet the board and administration were pulling in two directions. By the fifth year of no formal leadership and no vision, the school was in advanced stages of turf warfare and spiritual atrophy.

Second, the school had long since grown out of its current facilities. In fact, to accommodate the growth the previous headmaster had moved the fifth through twelfth grades to a separate campus in a former old bank building. This further added to serration, division, suspicion and misunderstanding within the ministry. The first thing I asked the board and administrative team to do when I arrived was to quickly read the book of John, read a biography on George Mueller, and expect God to do big things.

The first week I was at the school a group of board and administrators walked out onto our lower campus facility and I asked a very simple question, "What about consolidating the schools down here?" The silence was deafening. In this particular case it took someone from the outside to look at the situation and simply ask the obvious. There are many areas of school operations that require vision, faith, and courage. None is more important than praying for and developing a first-class physical plant for our children to attend the "Lord's School."

Special Learning Needs

Christian schools need to begin to evaluate the need for reaching out to children with special learning needs in their respective communities. There are a number of options in meeting the needs of at-risk children. Supplementary tutoring and pullout programs are viable in smaller schools with limited resources. Though effective, these programs can be time consuming and a cause of burn out for smaller schools that overstep their reach in terms of people and resources.

One important program that has crossed over the chasm and ministered quite effectively to children in special circumstances is the National Institute for Learning Disabilities (NILD). This program is "distinctively Christian," and "educationally unique." Here is "An Educators Perspective," taken directly from the NILD promotional literature.

Dear Educator,

Mary came to school today with a stomachache. She is facing a test. Although she is bright, she struggles just to pass. School has become a frustration for her.

Once Jeff longed to read. Now he approaches his reading group with embarrassment. The students will laugh at his mistakes.

You and I know these students. They sit in our classes. Instead of achieving, they meet with disappointment and failure.

How wonderful it was for me to have discovered the National Institute for Learning Disabilities (NILD).

Here was an organization dedicated to meeting the needs of students with learning disabilities. Sitting in the therapy stations, watching dedicated teachers relate to these students in a positive interaction, with exercises to quicken the minds of the children, I was convinced that God has raised up this special program to encourage parents, students, and educators alike.

Because of my enthusiasm to share with others the positive, beneficial aspects of the NILD program, I have listed some observations and suggestions, which may stimulate Christian school administrators to consider this effective program for students within their schools.

Observations

- A one-to-one ratio of therapists to students requires a strong board and administrative commitment.

- Every segment of the therapy session appears to be utilized profitably. The student benefits from the entire eighty-minute period twice weekly.

- Therapists display patience during the therapy sessions as they insist that students use good reasoning skills in arriving at appropriate conclusions in problem solving.

- A strong emphasis is placed on training the student to develop the ability to verbalize thinking processes.

During the therapy session a broad scope of important learning occurs such as:

- Improvement of verbal expression

- Emphasis on visual and auditory memory, discrimination and sequencing skills

- Correct responses to directions, stimulating auditory attention

- Development of proficiency in map skills, math computation, spelling, word attack skills, and handwriting

- Expansion of vocabulary
- Demand for accuracy in completing tasks for which the student has developed readiness
- Emphasis on improving directionality

Parents are trained to follow through significant aspects of the program with the child at home to reinforce particular skills. Parental limitations appear to be considered in giving assignments.

Suggestions

Christian school administrators

- Have you considered that every Christian school needs a program for students who learn differently?
- Have you asked your parents if they would be willing to fund a program?
- Have you contacted NILD for research validating this program?

Conclusion

Long-range solutions seem probable in the commitment NILD has to teaching toward the deficit. NILD philosophy centers on stimulating areas of weakness in perceptual and cognitive processing. Teaching LD students compensatory techniques that may employ "only the student's" strengths is not advocated. I recommend this program most heartily for your consideration. The answers it provides are life changing.

Sincerely,
Loreen Itterman, Ed.D
Former Associate Dean of Teacher Education
Columbia International University
Columbia, SC 9

Development

Every Christian school has a development office, whether they realize it or not. Parents and grandparents are the foremost means for financial growth and expansion that a school has. When Christian schools are in their infancy, the lead administrator must pray and seek the Lord's mind on how the future development of the school should proceed. The Christian school board has as its primary call a duty to live in the future. The school board sets the course for future growth. The lead administrator manages and leads that course of growth.

Development is, quite frankly, a misunderstood position in the Christian school movement. Development directors should never be given a cut of what they raise. The reasons are twofold. First, it compromises their ability to meet with people and not be benefiting personally, which would create a natural conflict of interest. Second, why would a development director be more valuable than the twenty year first grade teacher? Avoid the conflict and pay everyone a fair and just wage. Be creative in blessing people with cafeteria style benefits, rather than getting bogged down in the narrowness of salary and bonus discussions.

Development should include the establishment and management of the following financial areas of Christian school operations:

1. Endowment: The endowment is established to provide increasing principal growth, with an eye for allocating some interest spending in future years in designated areas. Those areas could include, but are not limited to, faculty study abroad, faculty graduate studies, seminars and conferences.

    Likewise the endowment could help fund student

financial aid, some program growth outside the normal budget, and so on.

2. Annual Fund: The Annual Fund is a series of fundraising experiences established to draw the school community together, establish new relationships with people outside the school family, and raise money to expand programs and support activities that are generally outside the auspices of the yearly budget.

3. Capital Campaign: The Capital Campaign is the most significant piece of the development office function. The Capital Campaign is typically a five to ten-year strategic pursuit of school-wide growth and expansion. The Capital Campaign requires intense board and administrative support. Capital Campaigns can also include a development or fundraising consultant.

The development director plays a big part in the introduction of the school to the community via local print and television coverage. A strong presence on the Web with a vibrant Web page is a must. Interpersonal focus on meeting and supporting local churches and pastors is essential. Naturally, membership in local civic organizations is valuable as well. In short, the development office can and should function in the smaller school through the lead administrator and board. In larger schools the development office must have clear job descriptions and measurable goals.

Finance

The finance department is the engine room of the Christian school. In smaller schools with the lead administrator and his wife handling the finances, it is important to call a board member in to help deflect some of the controversy that will no doubt come your way. Delinquent accounts suck the life out of Christian schools. When push comes to shove, parents pay their tuition bills last. In many cases the Christian school becomes a no interest loan center for families in financial trouble. Stop this practice immediately!

"I thought this was a Christian school." You will hear that refrain ten times if you hear it once. The answer is, "We are a Christian school; it requires money to operate this Christian school, and God has called us to be good stewards of the resources He has entrusted to us." The sooner report cards are held for delinquent accounts, the better off financially your school will be. Be prepared to minister to the needs of people in your school. Never be afraid of losing someone who is taking advantage of the school financially.

The finance department in small and large schools should be producing the following information on a regular basis:

1. Annual budget: Prepare this in November and finalize it in December. Revise the budget *once* in mid-September and go with it through thick and thin.

2. Fiscal Year: Christian schools should run their fiscal year, (the year designated in the budget) from July through June each year. It makes the best sense, since most of our new revenue begins with enrollment of students, from the spring and summer on.

3. Enrollment: Re-enrollment should begin in January for all returning families. February is for siblings of returning families that are not currently attending the school. March is then open to all new families. Schools with a church affiliation may wish to extend re-enrollment to April in order to include church families. The most important thing to realize is that it is far more cost effective to re-enroll an existing family than it is to go out and bring one in through advertising or gimmicks like discounts for existing families who recommend a new family to the school.

4. Daily Cash Reconciliations: Administrators must be able to see how much gas is in the tank at all times.

Cash reconciliations are daily reports of cash on hand in the school's accounts.

5. Weekly Profit and Loss (P&L) updates: These show in a microcosm the relative health of the school's finances relative to the budget. This also helps keep things in perspective, since schools typically are always on the verge of "needing" such and such in order to "survive."

6. Monthly P&L Statements: This formal document is the budget in a living, breathing format.

7. Yearly Audit: The yearly audit is a must for every Christian school, regardless of size. It promotes accountability, excellence and allows for ongoing education for the finance department in the latest laws and regulations affecting the Christian school. The superior Christian school, regardless of size, establishes strong financial controls from day one. Those failing to do so have already numbered the rest of their days.

PARENT TEACHER FELLOWSHIP (PTF)

Parent-run groups are either a major blessing or headache. To ensure the former, consider the following guidelines. First, the PTF is given a charter and developed directly under the authority of the school's governing board. The PTF should never be an autonomous body. The reason is the board and administration should always retain control over which types and how many fundraisers are presented to school families. Likewise, money can be a strange influence where not properly administrated. The administration should never be in a position to please people for financial inducements.

The best PTF organizations have clear lines of command and communication. Election of officers should be yearly with a three year cap on consecutive terms. Some people would scream, "Why?" The reason is simple; there are many ways to offer one's gifts to the Christian school. Someone truly desiring to serve would not be offended in the least with this arrangement. Someone vying for power or control might.

The best PTF organizations are entrepreneurs at heart. Here is one example. In a school I administrated, the PTF organized Christmas letters home to parents. The letters asked parents and students to offer money as a gift to each teacher, administrator, and aide or staff member they wished. The PTF then compiled the list, and wrote a nice letter to each faculty or staff member wishing them a merry Christmas. The PTF listed the names, but not the amount given from each family, and enclosed one check in the full amount given by all families to that teacher or staff member. Wow! What a blessing that was.

Other PTF groups ask parents right after acceptance into the school to prayerfully consider offering their professional or business services to the school paid staff at a deep discount. Here is how this works. A parent is asked to offer a lube and oil change for a year at 75 percent off the regular price. This is good only for paid faculty, staff, and administrators of the Christian school. It is not transferable or saleable.

Another example is a lawyer offering to cut 85 percent of his fee on closing costs on home purchases. A fast food restaurant owner could provide a special meal deal for up to two people for 20 percent of the regular price. How about a landscape maintenance owner providing 75 percent off his fee for basic lawn and garden care? The owner of a movie theatre kicked in up to ten dollars of free food and drink on every trip to the movies.

The key is the offer should be made to bless the staff. It should be better than a two for one or 50 percent off arrangement you can get on normal deals. The program is designed to supplement the typically low salaries and benefits Christian schools offer. It should represent the Acts church working and ministering together for the edification of the body. Our imaginations on something like this are our only limitations.

Those PTF groups that seek to serve are the best blessings. Selfless, Jesus-focused parent groups are the school's best advertisement. To build a seamless PTF, the first rate Christian school begins by having high expectations. Also, high standards of confidentiality, enthusiasm, and participation are essential.

CHAPTER eleven

Distinctive Excellence

> A disciple is not his teacher, nor a servant above his master.
>
> Matthew 10: 24

A distinctive excellence in the Christian school begins and ends with Jesus. Jesus is to be clearly exalted above everything and anything that comes into contact with the school. A stout refusal to allow anything to share the throne with Jesus is a signal that the excellent Christian school is growing in God's favor and strength. The following are some examples of distinctive excellence within the Christian school.

I'm Sorry

I'm sorry, please forgive me. This simple sentence will do more to model humility and servanthood than anything else you can say or do, period. Please use this often; it makes a difference in your life.

Recently I was called, as headmaster, to resolve a dispute between a parent, a teacher, and, by implication, our high school principal. The parents came in with both barrels loaded. They pointedly told me their daughter was being treated unfairly because of her race. They accused the teacher of being vindictive, and the principal of being indifferent and uncaring.

In listening to the parents, the teacher, principal, and I tried to be quick to listen and slow to speak. It was very hard to hear parents so upset with our school's treatment of their child. In the end I discerned that the child's infraction was in fact valid, and that the punishment was justified. I noted to all involved that the issue of the school's stance on race, student favoritism, and the like was irrelevant. The real issue as it pertained to the hurt evidenced in the meeting had *everything* to do with the manner in which we as a school approached the child's infraction.

I told the parents that I believed we had not handled the situation very well. The consequences of the child's behavior remained as administered by the teacher and the principal. The child needed to correct her mistakes. Next, the trauma caused by our well-intentioned, but misguided, efforts needed to be addressed. I began by saying I was sorry. The rest of the meeting centered on warm tears of relief, hugs, prayers, and profound thanks that they had been heard. The words *I'm sorry* heal many wounds.

THE MATTHEW PRINCIPLE

In any ministry people are the difference. People make or break a ministry. Parenthetically, Christians are just as prone, if not more so, to the malaise of gossip and slander. Proverbs 6:16-19 speaks directly to areas of interpersonal conflict that the Lord hates.

> These six things the Lord hates, yes seven are an abomination to Him:
> A proud look,
> A lying tongue,

Hands that shed innocent blood,

A heart that devises wicked plans,

Feet that are swift in running to evil,

A false witness who speaks lies,

And one who sows discord among the brethren.

Pride, lying, planning wicked acts, folks running to the "latest news," a false witness, and the person who deliberately sows discord within the body of Christ are hated by God. Unfortunately, these things run rampant in most Christian ministries. How are we to respond? The Bible gives clear instructions.

STOP: the gossip

PRAY: for the person

GO: to the person

STAND ON SCRIPTURE: Matthew 5:22–26, Matthew 7:1–6, Matthew 18:15–20

Practically, here is how to get victory in the Christian school ministry in the area of interpersonal relationships. First, establish a school culture of biblical confrontation. It is expected that you and I will be free to speak honestly and openly any time either of us are upset, offended, or hurt by the other. Second, teach the Proverbs 6 passage and how God hates it when we do what is written there. Third, teach and review often the Matthew Principle.

Every time a situation arises in our ministry, everyone in it understands there is a "system" for dealing with it. When someone comes to me with their issue, I simply tell them how much I love them and tell them to *stop* before what they say turns into gossip. Next I ask to *pray* for them. Finally, I encourage them to *go* directly to the person with whom they have the issue. Most people struggle with this step, but without it the seeds of hurt, frustration, anger, and bitterness become sowed, and the health of the ministry is then at stake.

The object of all biblical confrontation is restoration in right relationship with Christ. We all sin. We will all sin at some point against one another. Therefore when we do err it is necessary for our approach to be one of authentic love for one another. When our intent is to heal and not harm then we are well positioned to confront others with our concerns in a spirit of reconciliation and not condemnation.

Excuses

Don't use them. If you are complaining right now about this distinctive quality, you already have a problem. Excuses are those meddling verbal exchanges that occur with one intent in mind: to excuse poor or selfish behavior. The excellent Christian school has systems in place to deal with negligent or unproductive faculty and staff. It also uses systems to train children and to hold parents accountable. Excuses are a verbal form of rebellion against the authority to which the excuse is directed.

Examples of this are epidemic. The student may suggest he or she never heard, understood, or "got" the homework, final study sheet, etc. The misguided parent may state in emotional terms that "my child has many faults, but cheating is not one of them." The irresponsible teacher will state that they were late to school today because their child was sick, traffic was bad, their car had problems, or even "I just had a bad morning." Administrators use excuses too. "I left the minutes to the meeting in my briefcase. My day has been just too hectic."

Excuses demoralize the team. They also lower the standard of expected performance. The interesting thing about excuses is that everyone knows one when they hear one. Excuses are like poison. They seem to work effectively on the area used. The problem is you have to walk around the poison, can't touch it after you use it, and you need to worry about people, especially children, stumbling on it wherever it is stored. Save the stress, maintain your integrity, and avoid excuses like the plague. Again, establish workable policies and hold people accountable.

Lincoln Letters

Abraham fired his generals often. His secret was to simply fire them on paper in a letter he would pen, then let the letter sit in a drawer for a week or two. In most instances the letter written in the heat of anger, frustration, betrayal, or incompetence would read quite harshly. The purpose of the letters would be to let off some steam without acting rashly. Likewise, the letters allowed Lincoln to state clearly what was wrong and take time to evaluate it, if in fact the problems were as serious as he first suspected. We may consider the wisdom of this approach in our lives.

Lincoln letters help in faculty / administration conflict. They help in faculty / parent problems. They can be of great benefit in anyone's personal life. Lincoln letters can be used in virtually any area of interpersonal conflict. Using Lincoln letters help promote self-control may save a ministry, business, or personal relationship.

Eye Contact and a Firm Handshake

Administrators, board members, teachers, and aides should all understand the importance of a square look in the eye and a sincere handshake. Jesus was always out and about, walking and talking with people. He also touched people. All great leaders have a certain way with people. They find a way to connect. In general, it usually starts with strong eye contact and a firm handshake. Practice both.

BIRTHDAYS AND ANNIVERSARIES

The board or administration that takes time to remember and celebrate the birthdays of the faculty, staff and children in their Christian school is well on the road to a distinctive excellence. One way to celebrate the faculty, staff, board and administration birthdays and anniversaries is to note them in a weekly staff newsletter. To celebrate students' birthdays, the administrator could make post cards with his or her picture on it and mail a simple "Happy Birthday" to each child for his / her birthday. Likewise, students could be honored in homerooms, during chapels or assemblies, etc. The important thing is to do something.

HOMEROOMS IN GRAGES 6–12

Homerooms are a fun and simple way to build tremendous school spirit and improve school-wide communication. The best way to establish homerooms is to assign students one teacher for an entire year. The students meet three days a week in that homeroom teacher's room. Various school administrative details are handled in this situation. Class rings, class trips, test applications, homecoming information, etc., are handled in this setting.

One day a week the students meet in clubs. These include whatever the school supports. Examples include chess, art, drama, Future Business Leaders of America, and more. The participation in clubs is sure to skyrocket (which reminds me that a rocket club would be fun too). Making the clubs interesting and relevant is the key. Some clubs, like Odyssey of the Mind and Academic Decathlon, as well Honor

Societies, are highly competitive in their membership.

The other day of homeroom each week would be used for "home base." Home base is a time each week when the entire school gathers to celebrate the culture of the school. Birthdays, college acceptances, introducing art, music, speech, and sports champions are a big thrill in home base. Simple school-wide announcements such as cookie or magazine sales can be addressed. School-wide problems such as kindness, theft, or sloppy halls can be effortlessly addressed during home base. Home base is a time for surprises and joy. From time to time the school may also commiserate with and support a student or teacher who is going through a real crisis.

Dead Man Walking

Every day ponder the notion, "alive in Christ, dead in my flesh." Every day in every way I need to die to my flesh. Each choice I make every day needs to reflect the idea that I am not my own. Instead of things being "fair" for my child and me, I need to look for Christ in the trial, circumstance, or situation. The question is not, "How can I be served?" It is instead, "How may I better serve?" Watch out and be ready to be challenged as you step beyond the ordinary into the supernatural. We are not our own; we have been bought with a price. We are no longer alive in the flesh, but it is Christ who dwells within us. We are, in a sense, dead men walking.

We

In all we do, in each decision made, it is a "we thing." Though not everyone will agree with policies and direction in every instance, it is imperative that, in every instance, everyone supports the decision.

Unity, Harmony, and Love

We pray for this every day, often. It is what Jesus meant when he said, "Love one another." We encourage people to look for ways to express their love and appreciation for one another. One example is our "secret pal" program. Each summer during orientation we draw names from a hat and select our secret pal. We are given their birth date, favorite food, snack, Scripture, dream, etc. Throughout the year we pray for and bless our "pals." It is a wonderful surprise to be personally blessed when you least expect it.

You Know My Name!

There is no sweeter sound than when someone calls your name. Teachers do a great job knowing their students' names and something about them. Administrators should set as a goal to know the name of every child in their care as well. Impossible, you say?

That is the standard reply. However if someone really wanted to impact the children in a meaningful and powerful way, they would memorize the names and faces of all the children in their ministry. I am certain God would honor such an effort. By the way, I have a word of encouragement. When I was principal of a seventh through twelfth grade school with approximately 600 students, I learned each name and something about each child. It was a true blessing to sit with parents and surprise them with meaningful information on their child. It just isn't done these days. It is all the more reason for Christian school leaders to try to know their sheep.

A friend of mine shared this insight with me I believe may be helpful.

People do like to hear their names. I have a terrible auditory memory, and so I too felt that this was an impossible task. One of my teaching mentors showed me a silly yet effective way to memorize student names. You probably know this one. The teacher begins by introducing himself by name, and attaching a mnemonic device to his name (For instance, I'm Mr. Daly, and I'm worth nothing without my "daily" cup of coffee.) Then beginning at one end of the room, each student recounts the names and devices of each previous student before introducing himself or herself. By the end, almost everyone knows each other's name. Reluctantly, I have to admit that it works, even for me.

LIGHT TOUCH

> So likewise, whoever of you does not forsake all that he has cannot be my disciple.
>
> Luke 15:33

Listen carefully to me as I share something with you that is not normal. The ministry God has placed me in is not *my* ministry. It may be a shock to you, but we are serving the Lord and "the earth is His and the fullness thereof." We are borrowed for a season by the Lord to tend to the harvest He is bringing about. The moment I begin to consider that God has given me this ministry, it is a very short skip to the idea that the ministry God has placed me in is mine until He moves me on. Look out!

The idea of a light touch is in harmony with the biblical notion of being easily entreated. I am faithful and passionate about the ministry God has given me. I am not clingy, manipulative, or obsessed with the position to which He has assigned me. In this framework, I am available to be discipled or corrected, called or sent for His purposes. I am not tied to the whims of man.

The "light touch" allows you and me to boldly say and do

things for the Lord that otherwise are difficult simply because we are either afraid of offending or being offended. The light touch sets us free. Having a light touch on the ministry God has gifted us with encourages us to be free of disappointment, anger, and bitterness. Make a decision today to no longer be hostage to the whim of man.

Tell the Lord today you are prepared to forsake all to follow Him.

PLEASE AND THANK YOU

My grandmother told me I would always go farther with people if I used my manners. She also said something about getting more with an ounce of honey than a gallon of vinegar. *Please* and *thank you* are taken for granted today. More than ever they are a necessary ingredient in a healthy and holy Christian school system.

Some simple ideas for *please* and *thank-yous* include using the phrase "May I please …?" In staff or parent meetings slowly asking for something by saying please and smiling at the person is helpful. Try asking for someone's opinion with the words, "Would you please restate your view for me?" *Please* is the key that opens the door of understanding and respect. Use it often.

Thank you can be used in unlimited ways. Here are a few suggestions: thank you cards written to one or two faculty or staff members a week would do wonders for parent-faculty and administration-faculty relationships, surprise awards throughout the year in "public displays of affection" will boost morale throughout the school. Students love to see their teacher recognized in public for doing well. Candy bars, gift certificates, letters and notes, public blessings, and remembering birthdays and anniversaries are all ways of saying thank you. By far the most meaningful way to say thank you to those serving in and around Christian schools is to be honest, respectful, and fair with each and every person. Consistency and love are wonderful ways of saying please and thank you.

SHARE

It is a good idea to share everything we have with whoever may need it. Territorialism is unattractive. Sharing requires faith that God will replace what you have given or sustain you through what you are doing without. Share and share often. Sharing builds trust, love, acceptance, and a joyful spirit. Sharing is good.

FOLLOW ME!

> *You are to follow no man farther than he follows Christ.*
>
> John Collins
Puritan pastor

PRAYER

> Pray unceasingly.
>
> I Thessalonians 5:17

Prayer chains are important for every Christian school to have. Each person on the prayer chain is responsible for calling and praying with only two other folks. The speed and specificity with which a school can respond in prayer to a special need is dramatic and powerful. Daily prayer meetings with school leadership are essential. Weekly prayer summits with groups like Moms in Touch, or other parent-led groups are foundational to the health of the school. Prayer requests should be presented to school families and alumni at least weekly via e-mail or newsletter.

I Believe in You!

Say this more than once to someone and something special begins to happen in your relationship. I won't tell you what it is. Just try it for yourself and change the world!

You Can Do It!

Lovingly, truthfully, and consistently share this message with whomever you wish to deeply impact. The power of permission in the form of hope is beyond measure. When I owned a Domino's Pizza franchise, I met a man named Frank Meeks. Frank owned all the stores in Washington D.C. and northern Virginia. His stores at the time did more volume than any other franchise in the world. When I met him he shook my hand, looked me square in the eye and said, "You are going to make a terrific franchisee. You can be a millionaire! Take care of your people."

At a marriage of one of my former students, I passed a young man I had coached in baseball. As we exchanged hugs and pleasantries, I felt compelled to tell him, "God has gifted you in a strong manner in the area of business. You will do very well in business. Trust God in all you do." When I finished, he was stunned. He said, "Thanks Mr. Marsh, I have always wanted to go into business, but I didn't think I would be very good at it."

In both cases, the first with me being encouraged, and the second with me doing the encouraging, it is important to remember to do it. Too often stress and business prohibit us from reaching out in a very dynamic and meaningful manner in each other's lives. Change a life today and tell someone, "You can do it!" It may be the most important thing you ever teach, coach, or lead someone to.

By the way, I know you can do it! The Bible tells you so.

"I can do all things through Christ who strengthens me" (Phil 4:13.)

SHORT ACCOUNTS

Pray God will help you keep short accounts with those you minister with in the Christian school. Meet with people often. Ask people how you can better serve them. In proper settings ask folks if you have offended them and how you might make it right. When you are offended, take it to the Lord right away. Forgive the person and allow God to bring them around. Short accounts with people will allow you a longer life in Him.

NO

No. No? No! It doesn't matter how you say it; you simply need to learn to say it. No. No thank you. No, not at this time. No, I don't think it would be in our best interests now. Anyway you slice it, *no* is a powerful word. Those who choose to use it may experience discomfort initially, when people balk at its finality. Later, folks appreciate the clarity and consistency of someone willing to take a stand on something important to them. Learn to say no. Use it often!

GOOD TO GREAT

Good reports edify and testify. Give good reports as often as possible. People love to be blessed. Bless the people often. You may be blessed in return. You may also find people's performance tends to move from good to great when they are exhorted and spurred on to good works.

FAITH

I received this encouragement on faith in my box at school

one day from our director of development. It excited me. I hope it does you too.

How big is your God? What would have happened had Moses tried to figure out what was needed to accomplish God's command? One of the biggest arithmetical miracles in the world was required in the desert …. Now what was he going to do with them? They had to be fed, and feeding 3 ½ million people required a lot of food. According to the U.S. quartermaster general, Moses needed fifteen thousand tons of food a day, filling two freight trains, each one mile long. Besides, you must remember, they were collecting firewood to cook the food, not to mention for keeping warm. And if anyone tells you it doesn't get cold in the desert, don't believe it! Just cooking took four thousand tons of firewood and a few more freight trains, each a mile long. And this was only for one day!

They were forty years in transit! Let's not forget about water, shall we? If they only used enough to drink and wash a few dishes (no bathing?), it took 11 million gallons each day, enough to fill a train of tanker cars eighteen hundred miles long. And another thing! They had to get across the Red Sea in one night. Now if they went on a narrow path, double file, the line would be eight hundred miles long and require thirty-five days and nights to complete the crossing. So to get it over in one night, there had to be a space in the Red Sea three miles wide so they could walk five thousand abreast.

Think about this: Every time they camped at the end of the day, a campground the size of Rhode Island was required, or seven hundred and fifty square miles. Do you think that Moses sat down and figured out the logistics of what God told him to do before he set out from Egypt? I doubt it. He had faith that God would take care of everything.

LET US TAKE COURAGE; WE SHARE THE VERY SAME GOD!

CHAPTER

twelve

Technological Excellence

For as I was passing through and considering the objects of your worship, I even found an altar with this inscription: TO THE UNKNOWN GOD.

Acts 17:23

Technology can be unsettling. Technology use brings with it a tremendous responsibility. In its purest sense, technology is a neutral medium. Christian educators must educate themselves and their students to be active participants in the technology infrastructure of the new century. Christian educators must embrace technology. God is certainly big enough to guide each of us in the proper and meaningful use of new technologies.

E-MAIL

In the superior Christian school system every faculty and staff member is required to have an e-mail address. The head of the school should be corresponding weekly to the entire faculty and staff via e-mail. This is the twenty-first century; Christian schools must be way out in front to utilize existing technology in meaningful and efficient ways.

The Christian school that uses e-mail as part of its operating structure is sending a signal to families and the community that it is very serious about excellence. The model for children is also invaluable. Likewise, the faculty and staff in a Christian school using e-mail to communicate basic weekly information will acquire a sense of excitement, accomplishment, and school pride that is difficult to manufacture otherwise. The Christian school that is slow to implement this basic technology is seriously compromising the integrity of its academic focus.

The year after implementation within the faculty and staff, the Christian school should require the families attending the school to have at least one designated e-mail address to which the head of the school will communicate at least once a week. This must be communicated to families two to three years in advance of actual implementation. The faculty and staff are first, then the families. It is also important to request grandparents to be online too, if possible.

The benefits of using this new technology are many. Suffice it to say that it serves as a front line communication tool. Everyone will understand that everyone else receives the same correspondence in the same manner without student responsibility entering into the equation. The school should also use it to stop rumors when gossip begins to tear apart the fabric of trust in the school. Examples of this include dress code discussions, the perception that discipline is not being handled well, tuition hikes, and changes in personnel.

In brief, the use of e-mail will also translate into better faculty and student relationships. Students with questions or comments may correspond with their teachers and expect a response within a pre-specified time frame on any given day. This will be crucial to improving student performance through greater accountability and supervision. The uses are spectacular when it comes to students with special learning needs. Those students with extended sickness or on short-term mission trips also benefit in a new dynamic with the use of e-mail.

Personal Digital Assistants (PDA)

E-mail is the simplest form of system-wide use of technology in the excellent Christian school. The best part of using e-mail is that everyone has access to a computer to retrieve his or her e-mail messages. The next step in the technology focus is in the area of Personal Digital Assistants (PDAs). PDAs are going to be the foremost manner of communication within the next decade, if not sooner. PDAs will soon be in the form of wireless phones and a multiplicity of other innovations.

To give you a glimpse of the future, companies like Compaq, Ericson, Qualcomm, and others already market devices that are stretching the digital future. Some of the existing features include wireless e-mail and Internet. Telephone and scheduling capabilities are already married in a single hand-held device. Likewise, the ability to write, type, speak, and videoconference with one hand-held device is already available.

It sounds dangerous in a school setting, doesn't it? Before you dismiss out-of-hand the relevance of this technology in your school, consider this: the applications for excellence in your school are phenomenal. Imagine the use of this technology in a home-schooling program where the teacher teaches and is on real time video to the homes of home-schoolers, sick children, suspended children, and others.

Let's go a step further. How would you like your school, via the Internet, to draw students from fifty states and fifty countries? This technology affords that opportunity. The problem with expanding the reach of your ministry through technology is that your school will only grow as far as the leadership, faculty, and families are growing. It is up to the school leadership to determine the course of action that best fits the ministry vision of each school.

One strong word of caution is in order. Do not succumb to the notion that technology, in its present format, is not for you. If followed through to its logical conclusion, this is tragic and shortsighted. It is clearly time for Christian schools to take the high road in terms of the implementation and use of technology. Be mindful that the bar has been raised. Ask God to help your school meet and exceed the new standards of excellence in technology.

Web Page

All Christian schools should have a Web page. It is about as expensive as a yearly subscription to an academic journal. Web pages provide a whole host of opportunities for Christian schools. Suffice it to say that even if Christian schools don't have the time, resources, or talent to develop and host a Web page, it is still imperative that they acquire one. Eventually God will open up the eyes of understanding for each school and the unique God-breathed call to use the Web page for His glory. In the meantime, develop one so your Christian school will be ready when the marching orders come.

Web pages may be developed for a fee at many commercial web site developers. In most cases these web developers will help you design, implement, and host your new web site. The technology is unique and intriguing. It is also relevant and fun.

Homework Hotline

Develop a homework hotline in your Web page as soon

as you can. This single program will revolutionize your communication home to parents. Designate one person (for example the director of curriculum and instruction) or simply delegate the job to individual teachers in smaller schools. Each week the information is input onto your Web page. Parents simply log on at home and download the necessary homework. The idea that "I didn't know" or the teacher "never communicates to me" will be a footnote in educational history.

A similar usage is to communicate school calendar, handbook, curriculum, guidance, testing news, and so much more via your Web page. The opportunities are endless. Your imagination is your only limitation in the use of the Web page to draw your school community together in "A Classic Excellence."

CHAPTER thirteen

Traditions In Excellence

Seek to excel.

I Corinthians 14:12

This is by far the most enjoyable chapter for me to write. The ideas in this chapter are what make a first-class Christian school hum. When a Christian school has the time and ability to implement these ideas, the school is well on its way to national prominence and to establishing a classic excellence. Traditions in excellence start and end with a specific philosophy funneled through the school vision. It is in this manner that these traditions help weave unity, harmony, and love through the Christian school culture.

The first thing to note is that a school of any size can implement these items. Secondly, a school with minimum administration can and should implement the areas covered here. Third, this is just the tip of the iceberg. There are as many examples of excellence in the area of traditions as there are schools. Call a Christian school near you and compare ideas.

MANNERS

I was twenty-nine years old and had just been promoted

from part-time PE coach to school principal. I had never formally taught a full day of school in my life. I thought the professional teachers would get a kick out of hearing that. Likewise, I briefly considered the notion of sandbagging the parents at my first parent-teacher fellowship meeting. Somehow I must have had more teaching experience than half a year of rolling different balls out each day. I thought and thought; nothing believable came to mind.

The truth can be so boring. However, it is always the best choice. I asked God to help me speak in a coherent manner at my first big meeting. Somewhere in my upbringing I learned that first impressions are important. Unfortunately, I forgot about that lesson on this particular day. I wore shorts, sandals, and a Hawaiian shirt. The room was still as a summer's mist upon a black, moss-filled pond. I wondered if this was normal.

It wasn't. I was aware I had breached some unspoken law of etiquette. I wasn't sure what it was, but I was certain I had broken a rule. I wasn't concerned because God had given me a very specific vision for excellence in our school. That vision was entitled "Traditions in Excellence."

I explained to the parents my dilemma of never actually having taught a class. I shared how I had never operated a school of any kind. I thought it important to inform them of how little, in fact, I knew about anything having to do with a private Christian school. With that said, I shared the first areas of focus in our school for the upcoming school year.

First, no one would ever wear hats indoors. That included the gym, auditorium, and café. Second, no beanies, bandannas, or baggy pants. Third, we would dismiss ladies first from all classes, assemblies, and chapels. These three fundamental traditions permeated everything we did in every class every day. It made a tremendous impression on the students. Most notably, it promoted a sense of decency and order in all we did.

Next, teachers were required to train students to "stand and deliver" in class as they read passages from books, periodicals, current events, and the like. This helped students form a healthy respect for one another and for visitors; it also promoted good posture, poise, and increased reading scores.

Another etiquette concept is "speakers delight." Speaker's delight requires students to stand en masse the first time an adult addresses the student body in assemblies or chapels. This is straight out of Eton, circa 1780. People visiting the school using this tradition are universally impressed beyond belief.

A corollary to "speakers delight" is the notion of having a group of students called under-rowers. This group is responsible for hosting any formal guest to the school. These guests include chapel speakers, special assembly guests, visiting administrators and faculty, politicians, and so on. This group offers to pray for and answer any questions the visitors may have.

The notion of under-rowers comes from ancient Mesopotamia and other seafaring nations. Ships of old had men (usually slaves) in the bowels of the boat rowing with long oars. These under-rowers propelled the boat like an unseen force. Likewise, the Christian school needs "slaves" for Christ, to work selflessly as "unto the Lord and not man" in order to propel the school in the direction God has ordained.

In the classroom we also instituted a tradition called "class ambassadors." The teacher assigns class ambassadors in every class. The assigned student automatically greets visitors at the door without being prompted by the teacher, who is left free to continue teaching through interruptions.

The class ambassador introduces himself (or herself), the teacher, and subject matter. Then he or she briefly explains what is being taught, asks if the visitor would like prayer, and if the visitor has any requests of the teacher or class. This has been a tremendous tradition for excellence in our schools.

Walking the Talk

In the realm of fine and performing arts, one of the more essential traditions in excellence has to do with finding creative ways to share the gospel in a meaningful and specific manner. Including a salvation prayer on the back of program guides is one way to fulfill the Great Commission. Beginning each performance with a student testimony is another example of sharing the truth of Jesus. Clearly the music chosen and the scripts assembled need to reflect the vision of the school. Promotional banners creatively constructed to pique the reader's interest in Jesus and the production are an invaluable approach to introducing others to Jesus.

Athletics is perhaps the most vilified, yet potentially fruitful area for traditions in excellence to flourish. A few simple examples include the "fourth man in the fire." Taken from Daniel, this practice is a way to remind teams that Jesus is in the battle with them. It is signified by pointing all four digits from either hand into the air at the beginning of the fourth quarter or other crucial times in the athletic contest. The "wall of Jerusalem" is a tool whereby the fans at home games make a double-lined wall from the locker room door to center court in volleyball or basketball or mid-field in football. The purpose is to cheer real loud, and to encourage the team as they run through the wall. These activities all help build strong school and community spirit on behalf of the school.

"Cokes and tracts" is a tool we used to evangelize our opponents. At the end of every home game our players run to get a soda and a gospel tract to give the opposing player as they shake hands. In this manner, our students learn firsthand how to share their faith. In some instances people are uncomfortable with the practice. In that event, we are sensitive to their request. Each team also prays and hosts an out-of-town team to either a pizza party after the game or a sleepover if the visiting team is traveling from a far distance.

Senior farewells at the last home game of each sport season are a great way to reward students and bless parents and families. Seniors run from one end of the particular field of play to another with their father or designated male choice. The students run to their mothers and give Mom a red rose and big hug. Names are announced over loudspeakers, bullhorns, or whatever is convenient. Fine and performing arts seniors may also be included in these ceremonies, or a school may choose a separate venue to honor those students. Schools that include everyone find that rivalries are decreased between the arts, clubs, and athletics.

One word of caution as we discuss competitive areas of excellence. Too often the standards of the world creep into the program philosophies of Christian schools. It is important to remember that the most critical aspect of a superior Christian school extracurricular program is the fact that the expectations are very high in the area of personal effort. It is the effort of the students, not necessarily the results, that matters most. Talent will come and go, but the reputation of the school for strong effort will outlive any temporal accolades or championships that a school may garner.

Here is a simple story that speaks clearly to the power of effort in the field of competition.

A teenager lived alone with his father, and the two of them had a very special relationship. Even though the son was always on the bench, his father was always in the stands cheering. He never missed a game. This young man was still the smallest in the class when he entered high school. His father continued to encourage him but also made it very clear that he did not have to play football if he didn't want to.

The young man loved football and decided to hang in there. He was determined to try his best at every practice, and perhaps he'd get a chance to play when he was a senior.

All through high school he never missed a practice or a game, but remained a bench warmer all four years. His faithful father was always in the stands, always with words of encouragement for him.

When the young man went to college, he decided to try out for the football team as a "walk-on." Everyone was sure he could never make the cut, but he did. The coach admitted that he kept him on the roster because he always puts his heart and soul into every practice, and at the same time exemplified for the other members the spirit and hustle they badly needed.

The news that he had survived the cut thrilled him so much that he rushed to the nearest phone and called his father. His father shared his excitement and was sent season tickets for the college games.

This persistent young athlete never missed practice during his four years at college, but he never got to play in the game.

It was the end of his senior football season, and as he trotted out onto the practice field shortly before the big playoff game, the coach met him with a telegram. The young man read the telegram and he became deathly silent.

Swallowing hard, he mumbled to the coach, "My father died this morning. Is it alright if I miss practice today?" The coach put his arm gently around his shoulder and said, "Take the rest of the week off, son. And don't even plan to come back to the game on Saturday."

Saturday arrived, and the game was not going well. In the third quarter, when the team was ten points behind, a silent young man quietly slipped into the empty locker room and put on his football gear. As he ran onto the sidelines, the coach and his players were astounded to see their faithful teammate back so soon.

"Coach, please let me play. I've just got to play today," said the young man. The coach pretended not to hear him. There was no way he wanted his worst football player in this close playoff game. But the young man persisted, and finally, feeling sorry for the kid, the coach gave in. "All right," he said. "You can go in."

Before long, the coach, players, and everyone in the stands could not believe their eyes. This little unknown, who had never played before, was doing everything right. The opposing team could not stop him. He recovered an onside kick, blocked like a rhino protecting its young, picked up a fumble for a touchdown, and tackled as if the ball carrier was running away with the young man's every possession. His team began to triumph.

The score was soon tied. In the closing seconds of the game, this kid intercepted a pass and ran all the way for the winning touchdown. The fans broke loose. His teammates hoisted him onto their shoulders. Such cheering you've never heard!

Finally, after the stands had emptied and the team showered and left the locker room, the coach noticed that the young man was sitting quietly in the corner all alone. The coach came to him and said, "Kid, I can't believe it. You were fantastic! Tell me what got into you? How did you do it?"

The young man looked at the coach, with tears in his eyes, and said, "Well you knew my dad died, but did you know my dad was blind? The young man swallowed hard and forced a smile. "Dad came to all my games, but today was the first time he could see me play, and I wanted to show him I could do it."

Effort and heart promote standards that emphasize effort and heart.

BANNERS

Psalm 20:5 says, "We will rejoice in your salvation, and in the name of our God we will set up our banners. May the Lord fulfill all your petitions." Christian schools minister to children and young adults. Young people love to feel "part of something bigger than themselves." One way to build great traditions, school unity, school spirit and a sense of a bigger picture is to raise championship banners during homecoming week for the previous year's accomplishments.

The following are some specific ideas to help spice up the whole notion of banners. First, each school needs a philosophy of why and for what the banners are earned. For example, one rule of thumb could be any person or team that accomplishes a "championship that is recognized by either a national, state, regional, or league / conference organization would be eligible to earn a banner. Specific examples could include a state speech champion from your school, academic decathlon victors, surf team champions, basketball and field hockey league, and conference champions, etc.

The key in awarding banners to be hung in either the school gym or in lieu of a gym, the school café or hallways is to be fair game. Athletics will always be represented. Think outside the box. Include cheer champions, and spelling or poetry winners. How about All-State band winners? The list is endless. The key is to set clear expectations and high standards. Then celebrate the excellence the Lord has granted your school. Watch the enthusiasm in your school increase as a result.

One final idea on banners might help. Each school year ask coaches, team sponsors, and event advisors to pray and ask God if they might not have a specific Scripture that the Lord would use to guide and minister throughout that year's competitions. In the event a team or individual at your school is a champion, the Scripture becomes even more important. In addition to memorizing the Scripture throughout the season, the championship team would then place the Scripture on the championship banner itself. It becomes a wonderful memory as well as a terrific witnessing tool in future years. All banners should be designed and paid for by the current team parents for induction at the following year's homecoming.

SERVICE

Every Christian school grades three and up should have, as part of each year's matriculation requirement, service hours. Students should be required to serve a specific number of hours each year at the charity or activity of their choice. In the elementary school the classroom teacher keep a record. In the middle and high schools the homeroom teacher checks each quarter, and records the hours served. The hours should increase from, say, two hours a quarter in the third through fifth grades to three hours in the sixth through eighth grades and perhaps four hours in grades nine through twelve.

THE GREAT COMMISSION

Matthew 28:18–20 states: "Go therefore and make disciples of all the nations, baptizing them in the name of the Father and of the Son and of the Holy Spirit, teaching them to observe all things that I have commanded you; and lo, I am with you always, even to the end of the age."

Christian schools must have a meaningful and practical approach to evangelism. Jesus' own words command it. If our desire is to make disciples of Christ in our children, we must formulate an active strategy to follow His words, all of His words. For example, though many Christian schools are denominational, those that are not should passionately develop a clear non-denominational and inter-denominational philosophy of ministry.

Here are some examples directly from the mouth of Jesus. "Go ... preach ... baptize." How you and your school choose to implement these commands is up to you, (Sorry, only God can direct you in the tricky shoals of tempestuous Christian doctrine.) Another example is the Lord's Supper. Jesus tells us to do this "often in remembrance of me." (Luke 22:19, Matt. 26:26–28, Mark 14:22–24, 1 Cor. 12). How we choose to handle or ignore these simple yet powerful commands of Jesus will undoubtedly impact the lives of the people God has entrusted in the care of our ministries.

ACTS 1:8 A STRATEGIC PLAN FOR CHRISTIAN DYNAMISM

> But you shall receive power when the Holy Spirit has come upon you; and you shall be witnesses to Me in Jerusalem, and in Judea and Samaria, and to the end of the earth.

Christian schools wishing to practically integrate Matthew 28:18–20 and Acts 1:8 may consider the following blueprint. This strategic plan provides for mentoring, service, evangelism, and short-term missions. It can be a wonderful tool for exploring the words of Jesus.

The Jerusalem Project is scheduled for two days late in August. Jerusalem is considered our school property. Parents are mailed a list of needs for the school grounds and facility. On the appointed days, parents and their children come and serve the needs of the school together. Examples include weed pulling, grass mowing, curb painting, sign making, fence repair, and the like. Jerusalem project develops school pride, unity in the families and staff, and helps prepare the facility and grounds for the first day of school.

Judea Outreach is scheduled the week directly following outing week. Judea is considered our local town. The students in the same appointed grades go exactly one week later to serve ministries in the local community. These ministries include The Salvation Army, Christian shelter, Christian radio station, and more. On Monday the fourth and fifth grades may serve the Christian shelter. On Tuesday, the sixth and seventh grades may serve the Joseph House, a local orphanage and homeless shelter. The benefits of this outreach are as numerous as they are personal.

Samaria Evangelism is scheduled for a Friday in December. Samaria is our county or extended region. We contract with our local mall and ask to perform from 10:00 a.m. until 2:00 p.m. on a Friday in December. We bring our elementary and high school choirs to perform. Our worship team and drama teams also bring an evangelistic message. Additionally, those students and parents who have completed a witnessing training program together are also encouraged to hand out tracts and share their faith openly during our Samaria evangelism.

The **Ends of the Earth** is an ongoing effort to partner with our local churches. The ends of the earth for us is exactly that, anywhere God moves us. We advertise local church-sponsored missions trips, Israel trips, support opportunities, and more. Our students are expected as part of our school culture to involve themselves in some aspect of our Acts 1:8 vision. The local churches are blessed because of our added support. Students and families grow by leaps and bounds when challenged to meet Jesus at His words.

Books

Christian schools should develop reading lists. These reading lists should be completed on a regular schedule each quarter. Like service hours, classroom teachers and homeroom teachers check and grade students according to their satisfaction of these requirements. In both instances, students not completing the year's readings are not allowed to matriculate to the next grade. Seniors will not receive their diploma nor walk at graduation. Ideas for reading lists should include Mortimer Alder's Paideia "Great Works" list.

Outing Week

The first month of school each grade from grades four through twelve spends between one and three days on an "outing adventure." The younger students spend a day at a local camp, park, etc. The middle school students spend one or two nights at a Young Life camp or equivalent. The high school students spend two to three days on a campout type adventure.

The focus of outing week is two-fold. First, meet and draw closer to Jesus. Second, meet and draw closer to new and old friends. The fruit from this week, manifested throughout the year, is nothing short of profound. When people are given the time to meet and interact with one another, relationships become meaningful and distractions decrease accordingly.

Examples of trips include a hiking and river-rafting trip for eleventh and twelfth grades. Snow skiing trips for a day have been a big hit for the junior high. Campouts with rock climbing and canoeing have worked well for ninth and tenth grades. In every case the students are leading prayer, worship, and Bible studies. The adults are along to stop often throughout the experience and draw spiritual reflection out of the day's proceedings before the group heads back to the camp or lodge. Outing week helps to intensify the bonds of Christ and family in the Christian school.

Resurrection Week

Resurrection week is designed to occur around Easter. The first goal is to train our students to share their testimony within three minutes. Second, it is to afford those students wishing to share their testimony in a street-witnessing format. The beach, mall, local shopping center, and business park are all great places to allow students this wonderful opportunity.

Transportation is usually drop-off and pick-up by parents. Communication far in advance should placate most of the normal fears parents have about their child's safety. This is recommended for seventh through twelfth grades. Inviting local pastors, youth leaders, Bible school students, and parents adds to the excitement and intensity of the experience for the students.

During resurrection week students go out in small groups, usually by grade. The entire week has extended chapels.

Those students coming back are given the next chapel to share their experience. By week's end the enthusiasm and intensity of the students' experiences become overwhelming. It is fulfilling the Great Commission of Matthew 28:18-20, "Go therefore and make disciples of all the nations …"

Wilderness Week

Wilderness week is held the first week back from Easter break. Depending on the school, selected grades are given the opportunity to spend four days and three nights at a remote Christian camp. Highlights of the trip include the distance from home, great food, challenging rope courses, interesting team building games, daily Bible studies, and fantastic worship. This is truly designed to do for our children what Jesus did for Himself when He went away by Himself.

Homecoming BBQ and Bonfire

This week is BIG! The BBQ and bonfire are simply the culmination of a crazy yet meaningful week of traditions, games, testimonies and senior farewells. All students from the kindergarten on up are invited. Everyone wears his or her favorite school colors. Just about everyone sings, acts in a skit, plays games, participates in the longest "wall of Jerusalem" of the year, and rekindles old friendships. Grandparents are personally invited as well. The bonfire lights up at the very end while we sing worship songs. Afterwards, the younger children roast marshmallows.

Timothy Awards

This year-end Academy Awards style get together is the grand finale to the school year. Every child in the school will win an award this night. Students can only pick up their yearbooks on this date or on the beach, BBQ, and baptism date. The choir, drama club, speech club, worship teams and more have a showcase for the very best of what they did during the year. Artwork is posted in the foyer and championship banners are hoisted at this time. It is a very *big* deal. Normally, it is standing room only. It can be done, though it does take prayer and serious planning to make it "snappy, snappy" and not a drag.

Beach, BBQ, and Baptism

This is the sentimental favorite of all the students. Students may pick up their yearbook at Timothy Award night. Generally, no student is allowed to bring their yearbook to school until the last day of school at our Beach, BBQ, and baptism. We schedule games and competitions, as well as informal tournaments and free time for the students to sign yearbooks and say their good byes. During the last hour we worship, pray, and have a Bible study on baptism. Students are then given opportunity to be baptized. Parents and pastors are alerted in plenty of time to teach and pray their child through this public confession of a private commitment. It is an amazing time.

Uniforms (AKA Prescribed Wear)

Regarding uniforms. That is, to have or not to have. Consider this, you already have them. That is correct. Each Christian school has a minimum standard of dress. The question, then, is not, "To have or not to have uniforms." The question is to what degree a school will have prescribed wear. Each school will, no doubt, prayerfully consider the question in light of demographics, family input, and church or board wishes. Try not to overspend valuable time on this issue. Make a decision and move on.

Here are a few insights that may prove helpful. First, believe it or not, students would prefer a clear, consistent, and meaningful dress code. In grades K through eight the stricter the code the better. In grades nine through twelve solid reasoning behind the dress code is necessary. Also in grades nine through twelve consistent enforcement with clear consequences is absolutely essential.

One suggestion for a comprehensive policy would be as follows: All students will wear khaki pants to school. (Color of pants, shorts option in hot weather, skirts vs. pants for girls as an option, etc., can be discussed at your school). All students will wear either a short sleeve polo shirt or long sleeve oxford shirt. Sweaters will be crew neck in the following colors, (whatever your school desires.). Shoes will be brown leather.

One argument against a comprehensive "uniform" dress code is it stifles creativity or worse, critical thinking skills in the home. I believed both of these arguments for a number of years. That is until I sensed the Lord opening my mind to being creative in the following manner. Young people love to be different as they strive to conform. Though the clothing styles suggested above may sound preppy to some, there is a wonderful opportunity to lead students in a path of anticipation as they are given some freedom in the implementation of the policy.

Christian schools should encourage parents to meet the standard at any store of their choice. Some would order from Lands End. Others may shop at Marshalls or Ames or Wall-Mart and so forth. The key to this being successful, and a blessing to all is to contract with three or four embroidery shops in your town, who for a discount (because of volume), will sew your school's logo, mascot, or other moniker in one of three places on the shirts and sweaters of your students' prescribed wear.

Students would then choose to place the school's logo on the left sleeve of their oxford shirt, the left collar of their polo shirt or left chest of their crew neck sweater. The key is the school sets the standard for the type of dress. The parents and students then retain the creativity within limits of how to individualize their wardrobe. The school benefits by building greater unity, harmony, and the extra benefit in the community of daily advertising in the checkout line at the store, the baseball field before practice, etc.

One last insight regarding dress code: Consider spending at least one year prior to implementation of a prescribed wear policy discussing the issue with your school families. Address the cost and selection issue. Deal with the conformity issue. Share your school's special spin on the creativity issue. Build support and be enthusiastic. Once people feel heard and understand the *why* to this issue, they will support it and be blessed when you and your school clearly and consistently enforce it.

THE ROCK

Any school can find a big boulder or large rock to place on campus. The "Rock" is a wonderful tradition. Seniors are allowed to write, paint, or otherwise communicate to each other on the "Rock" throughout the year. It is a privilege only seniors enjoy.

During the week of homecoming, alumni are allowed to write on the "Rock." Likewise, during the final week of school, the seniors write their farewells to the juniors on the "Rock." The final week of school when the seniors are finished with finals, the juniors are allowed to "graduate to the Rock." This allows them to write for the first time on the "Rock" as they anticipate their senior year.

CHAPTER fourteen

Cost Of Excellence

Greater love has no one than this, than to lay down one's life for his friends.

John 15:13

LAY IT DOWN

The gospel is not a truth among other truths. Rather, it sets a question mark against all truths.

Karl Barth

Dietrich Bonhoeffer gave his life in pursuit of the gospel. He alone during the height of Nazi domination in his homeland of Germany opposed the intrusion of Hitler's politics within the country's churches. He would not compromise. He spent time in jail and died early, too early, as a martyr for Jesus Christ. Few people know that his first inclination was to flee the injustice rather than to stand and fight for what he believed was right. The following is a letter that helped him impact the cause of Christ in perilous times.

In 1933, Karl Barth wrote his discouraged colleague Dietrich Bonhoeffer who, disgusted with the German Christian response to Hitler, fled Germany to pastor a

German-speaking parish in England.

"What is all this about 'going away,' and 'quietness of pastoral work," etc., at a moment when you are wanted in Germany? You, who know as well as I do that the opposition in Berlin and the opposition of the church in Germany as a whole stands inwardly on such weak feet!...Why aren't you always there where so much could depend on there being a couple of game people on the watch on every occasion, great or small, and trying to save what there is to be saved?...

"I think I can see from your letter that you, like all of us—yes, all of us!—are suffering under the quite common difficulty of taking 'certain steps" in the present chaos, that we are rather required in and with our uncertainty, even if we should stumble or go wrong ten times or a hundred times, to do our bit?...

"One simply cannot become weary now. Still less can one go to England! What in all the world would you want to do there?...You must now leave go of all these intellectual flourishes and special considerations, however interesting they may be, and think of only one thing, that you are a German, that the house of your church is on fire, that you know enough to be able to help and that you must return to your post by the next ship."

Bonhoeffer returned to Germany sixteen months later, after Barth had been exiled to Switzerland.[10]

In Christian education teachers, aides, administrators, and churches must lay aside individual and institutional desires and support completely the move of God within the Christian school movement. Christian schools are arguably the most important evangelization and discipleship tool the

Lord is using to rescue and raise up the next generation of godly leadership. Why wouldn't churches financially support Christian schools as they do missions? Why wouldn't politics as usual in Christian schools cease, in favor of a Christ centered focus on love, relationships, and service to one another?

It is time for people in Christian education and on the periphery of Christian schooling to "lay it down." Lay down the personal agendas. Lay down the religious expectations. Lay down the selfish self-promoting. Lay down whatever is not purely Jesus. Seek Him and Him alone.

BELIEVE

Christianity, if false, is of no importance, and if true, of infinite importance. The one thing it cannot be is moderately important.

C.S. Lewis

Who do you say that I am?

Jesus Christ.

Believe God for big things in your ministry. George Müeller did! Basil Miller writes in his biography on George Müeller.

Mr. Müeller's faith was so dominant that however much the need, he rested calmly in the divine assurance that God's hand would contain a bounteous supply when the moment arrived. He and worry parted forever. Though he was deeply concerned, he never fretted at delay in receiving answers to his requests.

On February 15, 1842, his attitude is typical. "I sat

peacefully down to give myself to meditation over the Word, considering that was now my service, though I knew not whether there was a morsel of bread for tea in any one of the houses, but being assured that the Lord would provide. For through grace my mind is so fully assured of the faithfulness of the Lord, that in the midst of the greatest need, I am enabled in peace to go about my other work. Indeed, did not the Lord give me this, which is the result of trusting in Him, I should be scarcely able to work at all.

March 19 began in poverty and dire need, only seven shillings having come in during three days. "There was not one ray of light as far as natural prospects." So Mr. Mueller proposed to his workers that the day be set for prayer. When they met at ten thirty, immediately by three separate people twenty-one shillings were brought in. They called a similar session of prayer for the evening, for there were yet three shillings lacking. Before the evening service was over the three shillings had arrived, plus an additional three.

In giving advice gained through daily trials of his faith, this father of orphans laid down rules for Christians to follow by which they might strengthen their faith. These rules are:

1. *Read the Bible and meditate on it. God has become known to us through prayer and meditation upon His own Word.*
2. *Seek to maintain an upright heart and a good conscience.*
3. *If we desire our faith to be strengthened, we should not shrink from opportunities where our faith may be tried, and therefore, through trial, be strengthened.*

The last important point for the strengthening of our faith is that we let God work for us, when the hour of trial and our faith comes, and do not work a deliverance of our own.[11]

DREAM BIG!

I have a dream my four little children will one day live in a nation where they will not be judged by the color of their skin but by the content of their character.

Martin Luther King, Jr.

Set an example in your ministry for the children, faculty, staff and parents to follow. Dream big and often. Hope for God's best. Be positive and alert. Allow God to do wonderful things in your life and the life of your ministry. Dream big!

PAY THE PRICE

By January 1956, with the Montgomery bus boycott in full swing, threatening phone calls, up to 40 a day, began pouring into King's home. Though he put up a strong front, the threats unsettled him. One midnight as he sat over a cup of coffee worrying, the phone rang again, and the caller said, "Nigger, we are tired of you and your mess now. And if you aren't out of this town in three days, we're going to blow your brains out and blow up your house." King later described what happened in the next few minutes:

I sat there and thought about a beautiful little daughter who had just been born .... She was the darling of my life. I'd come in night after night and see that gentle little smile. And I sat at that table thinking about that little girl and thinking about the fact that she could be taken away from me any minute.

And I started thinking about a dedicated, devoted, and loyal wife, who was over there asleep. And she could be taken from me, or I could be taken from her. And I got to the point where I couldn't take it any longer. I was weak ....

And I discovered then that religion had to become real to me, and I had to know God for myself. And I bowed down over that cup of coffee. I will never forget it ... I prayed a prayer, and I prayed out loud that night. I said, "Lord, I'm down here trying to do what's right. I think I'm right. I think the cause we represent is right. But Lord, I must confess that I'm weak now. I'm faltering. I'm losing my courage. And I can't let the people see me like this because if they see me weak and losing my courage, they will begin to get weak ...."

And it seemed at that moment that I could hear an inner voice saying to me, "Martin Luther, stand up for righteousness. Stand up for justice. Stand up for truth. And lo I will be with you, even until the end of the world.... Almost at once my fears began to go. My uncertainty disappeared."[12]

SHAKE IT OFF AND STEP UP

A parable is told of a farmer who owned an old mule. The mule fell into the farmer's well. The farmer heard the mule "braying" or whatever mules do when they fall into wells. After carefully assessing the situation, the farmer sympathized with the mule, but decided that neither the mule nor the well was worth the trouble of saving.

Instead he called his neighbors together and told them what had happened ... and enlisted them to help haul dirt to bury the old mule in the well and put him out of his misery.

Initially, the old mule was hysterical! But as the farmer and his neighbors continued shoveling and the dirt hit his back ... a thought struck him. It suddenly dawned on him that every time a shovel load of dirt landed on his back ... he should shake it off and step up! This he did blow after blow.

"Shake it off and step up ... shake it off and step up ... shake it off and step up!" he repeated to encourage himself. No matter how painful the blows, or distressing the situation seemed the old mule fought panic and just kept right on shaking it off and stepping up!

It was not long before the old mule, battered and exhausted, stepped triumphantly over the wall of that well. What seemed like it would bury him actually blessed him ... all because of the manner in which he handled his adversity.

That's life! If we face our problems and respond to them positively, and refuse to give in to panic, bitterness or self-pity ... the adversities that come along to bury us usually have within them the potential to benefit and bless us!

Remember forgiveness-faith-prayer-praise and hope.... All are excellent ways to "shake it off and step up," out of the wells in which we find ourselves!

One more thing ... "never be afraid to try something new. Remember, amateurs built the ark. Professionals built the Titanic."

Author unknown

The Man in the Arena

In the Christian school movement there will always be critics. Generally, these critics will have a "form of godliness but denying its power. And from such people turn away" (2 Timothy 2:5). In a spiritual sense, we must understand it is the Enemy, the Great Deceiver, Satan himself who is behind the critical spirit. The reason for the criticism varies depending on the issue at hand.

Suffice it to say, criticism will surface when it is least convenient. Therefore, before the criticism begins, we must prepare our hearts and minds. Prayer, Scripture reading, and teaching our faculty and staff how to properly handle criticism is critical to diffusing the critical spirit and its cousins: gossip, slander, and discord. Again, our school culture must openly address the *when* of criticism so we may *win* the battle of criticism through a humble and contrite spirit.

Please understand in most cases the person with the critical spirit simply feels left out. They are generally afraid of the change being contemplated. Their faith is weak or non-existent. They also may be afraid of losing influence or position. The only solution for you and me is to obey God. Love the critic, pray for them, and explain once what you feel God telling you to do, and then move on … next.

Critics are notorious for ministry skipping. They are the ones who initially come to you and say how great your ministry is compared to "so and so's" ministry. Flattery goes hand in hand with the critical spirit. Once ensconced in your ministry without proper training and accountability, the poison of the critical spirit begins to flow. Regardless of how they arrived in your ministry, a proper perspective is essential.

Theodore Roosevelt wrote an essay called "The Man

in the Arena." It provides a clear perspective for those in ministry, for those in the "arena."

It is not the critic who counts, not the one who points out how the strong man stumbled, or how the doer of deeds might have done them better. The credit belongs to the man who is actually in the arena, whose face is marred with sweat and dust and blood ... who, if he fails, at least fails while daring greatly, so that his place shall never be with those cold and timid souls, who know neither victory nor defeat.

Chapter Fifteen

Eternal Excellence

And whoever receives one little child like this in My name receives me.

Matthew 18:5

In the Christian school it is important to keep first things first. There are so many competing influences that a school whose leadership is not focused squarely on the Lord is in constant danger of losing touch with God and His plan for the school. Here are some random meanderings on the importance of staying close to God.

First, God's gifts and calling are irrevocable. This should give you confidence in life in spite of opposition. God's call gives security as a member of His body. God's call is different and unique; it can't be counterfeited by the Devil.

Second, God's will is a daily process. It requires abiding in Him. Relax. Let things go. Take your fingerprints off God's handiwork. He did fine without you. Read His Word, pray often throughout the day, fellowship with other likeminded Christians. Be aware that fleeces are sometimes too easy to manipulate. Rather rely on Gods continuing to lead in your life; be surprised by His perfect will that will be perfect for you.

Third, concerning decision-making, Viggo Olsen's model is as good as any. "Erase and pray." That is, forget the troubles concerning your immediate circumstances and pray for a fresh touch from God. Read and remember, i.e. read the Bible and recall all God has done in your past to remind you of His faithfulness. Next, consider and think of the options, what you have read in the Bible, your circumstances, and where faith and God's glory fit in. "Decide and check" is the final stage of biblical decision-making. When you are faced with God moving in your life on a daily basis, you will eventually arrive at a point of decision. Simply "decide, then check" to ensure that the decision is what you had planned. Look for fruit of God's Spirit in the decision and then move on.

In his work *Experiencing God*, Henry Blackaby paints a practical model of "knowing and doing the will of God." Blackaby suggests God is always at work around you. It is God who pursues a continuing love relationship with you that is real and personal. God then invites you to become involved with Him in His work. We then understand that God speaks by the Holy Spirit through the Bible, prayer, circumstances, and the church to reveal Himself, His purposes, and His ways.

God's invitation to work with Him always leads you to a crisis of belief that requires faith and action. You must then make major adjustments in your life to join God in what He is doing. Finally you come to know God by experience as you obey Him and He accomplishes His work through you.[13] This simple yet profound format for understanding God's will in the life of a school and its leadership is well worth noting. Remember one last item in spiritual decision-making. God gives us weakness or allows attack in our lives in order to draw us closer to Him.

Dr. Janet Lowrie Nason writing in *Christian School Education* sets forth in clear terms "Selected Indicators of a Healthy Spiritual Culture in the Christian School":

BOARD MEMBERS

- Are elected because of their spiritual leadership, not their giving potential
- Prioritize time spent in the Word at home and at regular board meetings
- Address interpersonal conflicts in a godly way, practicing kindness and humility
- Practice exercising "true religion" in determining policies that impact single-parent families in the school family
- Pointedly ask, How does God want us to exercise faith this year in our school? And take action steps accordingly
- Determine Bible-centered positions after prudent research, market surveys, and consultant information; where differences are evident, choose God's truth over the world's wisdom
- Pray daily against the spiritual forces of evil that are fighting over the souls of the children who are the next generation of godly leadership
- Value the teachers, who are the school's largest donors in that they work for far less than they would earn elsewhere; act when possible to raise salaries and benefits, recognizing that a workman is worthy of just wages
- Steadfastly practice the Matthew 18 principle by gently and firmly sending complaining parents and teachers to the administration according to the biblical model
- Nurture a biblical and global perspective on God's work in Christian schools; allocate funds to help needy children in international Christian schools; encourage teachers and administrators to travel and report on how the money has been used strategically in another culture

- Define the parameters of the school's constituency, recognizing that only a school with unlimited resources could teach all children with varied learning needs, and it is not "un-Christian" to limit admissions in order to protect the school's integrity and carry out its defined mission

- Seek God's wisdom for the future through a cycle of evaluation and revision, and through long-range planning at one-, five-, and ten-year intervals carefully review new parents in accordance with the school's spiritual admissions policy

- Study the Word and school law, and do what is right in hiring and releasing school personnel

- Provide through their own families godly models of Christian homes

- Practice personal integrity, never violating policy or the Word to manipulate decisions

Administrators

- Exercise authority as a servant-leader, purposefully avoiding pride, which clogs the Holy Spirit's work

- Constantly evaluate the spiritual pulse of the school to ensure against developing lukewarm Christians who have a form of godliness but no power

- Use their position as a "change agent" to modify programming in order to raise children who are pleasing to God

- Spiritually encourage the school family in practical ways

- Develop proactive ways of identifying and handling "at risk" children before crisis management is needed

- Propose fiscal policies that enable parents to meet their financial responsibilities to the school

- Seek daily spiritual direction from the Word, recognizing that administration is emotionally and spiritually draining

- Know that "knowledge puffs up, but love builds up"

- Confront pathology in the body such as "scorners and mockers" and "wild power centers"; if change is not evident, take steps to remove them according to biblical directives

- Demonstrate credibility in the way they say yes and no, and in keeping their word even to their own detriment

- Pray for emotional and physical strength, recognizing that administrators will be misunderstood because confidentiality sometimes prohibits explanations; trust God alone for their reputation

- Actively guard against sexual temptation in all forms; step out of spiritual leadership if moral failure occurs

- Develop leadership in subordinates by delegating tasks with accountability steps, just as Jesus did with His disciples; understand that micromanagement is usually a pride or insecurity issue

- Refuse to be threatened by promising subordinates and encourage their professional and spiritual growth

- Work through personal pain in biblical ways instead of through denial or addictive behaviors

- Give advance notice of upcoming change, modeling Jesus

- Arm for the daily spiritual battle, preparing for the war that occurs on a regular basis in the Christ-centered school

- Cultivate healthy personal activities, and step away from the school's stress and discouragement

- Realize that personal suffering is a true blessing in

that it is the key to understanding Scripture and gives administrators credibility in ministering to hurting Christians

Parents

- Maintain strong Christian homes, understanding that Christian schools cannot compensate for weak ones, but work best with healthy ones.
- Love and esteem their spouses, modeling Christ's love for the church by practicing sexual purity.
- Pay school bills on time, demonstrating biblical responsibility.
- Refuse to undermine the authority of teachers and administrators by criticizing them in front of children.
- Pray daily for teachers, staff, and coaches who interact with children.
- Tangibly encourage with creative "cups of water" offered in Jesus name.
- Follow the Matthew 18 principle by talking directly with the one who has caused the perceived problem as soon as possible.
- Be diligent and consistent in disciplining children in order to teach parental obedience, the prerequisite for obeying God.
- Be courageous in facing and intervening in destructive behavior of hurting children.
- Discipline yourself to ask, *How would Jesus cheer from the sidelines or bleachers of this athletic event?* Then act accordingly.
- Practice the same patience Jesus did while repeatedly answering the same questions from His disciples, who were grown men.

- Model and teach support of the school dress code by avoiding gray areas or the "appearance" of questionable clothing.

- Ask forgiveness when you have wronged others.

- Seek ways to demonstrate a generous spirit in practicing true religion by helping single parents with such matters as transportation and child care.

- Refuse to participate in any "wild power center" that undermines the school's authority structure.

- Demonstrate to children how Christians move out of comfort zones to lift up Jesus Christ.

- Teach children that God answers prayer according to His timing and His will.

- Instruct children that sexual abstinence before marriage is biblical and builds the strongest marriages.

- Look for ways to show children how to care for others in practical ways.

- Define success not by how much money children can spend but by how they are spending it.

- Articulate to children that God can and will finance His will for their lives.

- Refuse to be drawn into "roots of bitterness" where many are defiled.

Teachers

- Evaluate the spiritual climate of the classroom by being aware of class dynamics and interrupting the planned curriculum to deal with problems and facilitate forgiveness when necessary.

- Maximize the role of the Holy Spirit in the teaching and learning process.

- Generously show love to others instead of dispensing it as a limited commodity.
- Practice kindness, tenderheartedly forgiving others.
- Exhibit a healthy model of the body of Christ, knowing that children watch and learn from the daily interaction of adults.
- Be spirit-controlled at all times.
- Constantly ask, *How would Jesus teach and administer justice and mercy in this classroom?*
- Pray for courage in discussing student problems with parents.
- Ensure that testing, records, and lesson plans are orderly and accessible.
- Physically demonstrate the joy of the Lord by consciously looking and smiling at students in such areas as the hallways, recess area and gym.
- Retreat to the mountains or other locations to be led by "still waters" for restoration of soul, and an awareness of personal human limitations.
- Find identity and significance in Jesus Christ, not in a codependency relationship with the school.
- Guard against immorality or sexual temptation, including pornography.
- Discipline their lives to have a healthy, growing relationship with Jesus Christ.
- Discern when a student is under spiritual conviction in order to lead him or her to salvation or recommitment.
- Draw strength from the "emotional scars" of past pain as they represent God's grace and power.
- Say no to worthy Christian causes in church and para-church organizations in order to meet their primary

responsibilities in home and school.

- Identify manipulative devices of dysfunctional people who try to influence and control behavior through guilt, assertiveness, or position; discern godly ways to deal with them by setting personal boundaries.
- Practice sending "flare prayers" during emergencies such as confrontations with irate parents, loss of electrical power, and playground accidents."[14]

To this group I would add a section on students.

STUDENTS

- Be willing and open to following Jesus Christ in their lives.
- Be called of God to attend the Christian school.
- Be prepared to "give a defense for the hope that is within them."
- To be easily entreated and open to correction and rebuke.
- Love the school and desire to change those things that are outdated, irrelevant or without meaning, in ways that encourage and build up not tear down.
- Be willing to say "I'm sorry please forgive me."
- Have a strong respect for authority and a willingness to obey, even if a certain policy or procedure is seemingly random and ineffectual.
- Be diligent to complete homework assignments.
- Be faithful to complete class projects.
- Be truthful to avoid the temptation of cheating.
- Be prayerful to ask God to help overcome the temptation of sexual impurity and alcohol and drugs.
- Be careful to develop a strong witness in Christ so

younger students will have a strong role model to look up to.

- Have an adventurous spirit to participate in school trips, missions, and the like.
- Give back to the school and community by exercising their gifts freely for the Lord.

In Christian schools there will always be people who go to church, tell you they are saved, are as kind and thoughtful as can be, and are in fact going straight to hell. The irony in many cases is that these same people can be the school's greatest supporters. It is imperative that the school leadership be honest about the reality that God will send people to the school and, in some cases, allow people in leadership who are not yet saved. Of course, there are other people who will know just enough about the things of God to sandbag the admissions committee or whoever is interviewing them. These people are untruthful and also need a Savior.

There are also instances where, unknowingly, someone may be hired on staff and not really know Christ as Savior. This would seem to be tragic, and is if left unresolved. Instead of pretending, it is imperative that the school leadership pray and address the need for salvation with the staff member in question. Though this may seem far-fetched, it is really quite common. Likewise, we need to understand that on a good day we may have 50 percent of our students saved. Our job in Christian education is not to guess who is and isn't saved. Rather, our job is to present the living gospel of Christ in everything we do. Everything!

In one school I was administering I had just been hired. During the summer orientation, I preached the gospel of Christ as a means to encourage faculty and staff to share with their students. After the third day, one aide and two teachers accepted Christ as Savior. Later in the year we were able to explain salvation to one board member and minister assurance of salvation to another. Be open and available to God's leading; obey when He shows you someone in need of Him, regardless of their position or place in the school.

Greg Laurie, the international evangelist from the Harvest Crusade ministries, put out a relevant and insightful piece on evangelism framed in the context of the Titanic movie success of a few years ago. Here is what he said in his "Lessons from the Titanic."

It was the greatest maritime disaster in human history. Some had said of the Titanic, 'Even God Himself couldn't sink it.' But on April 14, 1912, just five days into its maiden voyage, the Titanic went down, taking fifteen hundred people to an icy grave.

Countless thousands are hearing this dramatic story for the first time through the film ***Titanic***. *It is now the highest box office draw of all time. Many people have gone to see it repeatedly, enthralled by its story, moved by its characters. Why has it gripped the world's imagination for 85 years?*

The ship of dreams

Perhaps the story of the Titanic looms larger than life because it was the "ship of dreams." This massive ship, the largest and most luxurious of its day, was a grandiose symbol of its time. People held a buoyant optimism about the future. A new philosophy for living was emerging. The new century had just dawned and man was going to build a "heaven on earth."

The thought prevailed that perhaps mankind could "best nature" and "even God" through technology. As a result, when the Titanic was built, nothing was spared.

It harnessed all of the latest technology; it was filled with luxurious staterooms and elegant dining halls. And when it was finished, people called it "unsinkable."

The millionaire special

It seemed that everybody of stature wanted to be a part of its maiden voyage. So many millionaires were on board that it was dubbed "The Millionaire Special." The combined wealth of its passengers equaled $500 million (multiplied billions in today's economy)!

The ship's passenger list included some of the world's wealthiest people. John Jacob Astor, whose fortune was estimated at $150 million, was returning from a trip from Egypt with his new nineteen-year-old bride. Benjamin Guggenheim, valued at $95 million, was on board with his mistress. Isadore Strauss, founder of Macy's department store, worth $50 million, secured passage, as did Jay Ismay, with an estimated wealth of $40 million. Today's counterpart would be to set sail on a cruise with Ross Perot, Bill Gates, Steve Forbes, Steven Spielberg and Donald Trump.

"Shut-up, shut-up, we're busy!"

Most of us are familiar with the sinking of the great ship. There were repeated warnings of icebergs ahead. One ship, the **Californian**, *sent the message via Morse code, "I say, old man, we are surrounded by ice!"*

The reply from the Titanic was both tragic and telling. It wired back, "Shut-up, shut-up! We're busy!"

Despite repeated warnings (seven in all), the Titanic sped ahead until it hit an iceberg that tore a 200-foot gash in its side. But when the passengers were instructed to get into the lifeboats, they failed to take the danger seriously. Some just went to bed, confident that the Titanic would be fine. Many of the passengers just laughed it off drinking, dancing, gambling and partying the night away. One person grabbed some broken chunks of ice from the iceberg saying, "Get me another one for my drink!" Others took hunks of ice back to their staterooms to show their friends when they arrived in New York City.

Still others put their life preservers on and danced around the deck while onlookers laughed. Some refused to put the life jackets on because they didn't want to dirty or wrinkle their expensive clothes.

Room in the lifeboats

The ship's stewards literally broke into staterooms in order to rouse people from sleep and warn them of the peril. Most passengers simply couldn't believe that this unsinkable ship could actually sink! Because of their disbelief, lifeboat after lifeboat pulled away from the ship with only ten to fifteen persons on board, though they had the capacity of up to sixty. When a series of loud explosions rocked the ship, it awoke the people to their impending doom, and panic ensued as they stampeded toward the remaining lifeboats.

Money can't buy you life

There are many ironies associated with this tragedy. Chief among them was that many of those who perished on the ship could have "bought" the ship. But their money was not enough to secure just one seat on a lifeboat. Imagine those men and women standing on the decks—some draped in the finest furs that money could buy, others with rings on their fingers, pearls around their necks, diamond earrings in their ears and diamond tiaras in their hair. Yet, at that moment, their lives counted for no more or less than the poorest steerage passenger. One first-class passenger, realizing his fate, went to the side of the ship and dumped out all his money. Through it all, the band played on until the final, horrible end.

The Titanic's message today

If there is a message in the sinking of the Titanic, it may be that man has turned a deaf ear to his fate. While the world around us sinks, we choose to believe that everything is going to be all right. But is it? Should we "party" our lives away and forget that something called death is inevitably coming? It has been said that the statistics on death are quite impressive: one out of every person dies.

You may be caught up in pursuing a career right now, chasing that elusive raise or that valued promotion. You may be hoping that once you reach that certain plateau, you will finally be "happy." But will you? What good was all the wealth of those who died that night in the icy Atlantic? Of what value was all that money when the ship was sinking?

Life can be like the Titanic

The "Titanic" we've booked passage on can come in the form of careers, relationships, and even religion. But, one day, those ships will sink, and like the passengers aboard the Titanic, we will face eternity. Life for *everyone—be they the most famous person or the least heard of—must eventually come to an end.*

God has provided a lifeboat for you!

But God has provided a lifeboat for mankind. It is found in a relationship with Him through His Son, Jesus Christ. You see, we are all separated from God by our sin, be it intentional or unintentional. The Bible tells us, "All have sinned and fallen short of the glory of God." There is not a single exception to that statement. Every Titanic will sink!

That is why some two thousand years ago, Jesus Christ, the Son of God, died on a cross for our sin. He personally paid the price for the sins we've committed.

Jesus said, "For God so loved the world that He gave His only begotten Son, that whosoever believes in Him (trusts in, clings to, relies on) should not perish, but have everlasting life." Just as those passengers on the Titanic entrusted their lives to a lifeboat to keep them from an icy grave, so, too, we must entrust our lives to the "lifeboat" of Christ.

How to get on board

In fact committing your life to Christ can be compared to being on board the Titanic. As the water floods the decks, you realize you have only moments to decide. Before you a lifeboat is waiting. You have a choice: get into the lifeboat and live, or stay on the titanic and die.

You might say, "I'm undecided! I'll just stay here and think about it for awhile." But to do so means certain death. Either you leave the Titanic for the lifeboat, or you stay on and go down.

The same is true of becoming a Christian. You either are one—or you are not. Jesus has said that we are either for Him or against Him. To be undecided is to be decided—decidedly against Him.

Do you want to get into God's lifeboat?

Do you want to be prepared for eternity?

Do you want to find the meaning and purpose of life?

Do not foolishly say, like those on board that night, "Shut-up, shut-up! We're busy!" Take these steps and secure your passage to eternity.

1. Realize that you are a sinner.

No matter how good a life we try to live, we will still fall miserably short of God's standards. The Bible says, "No one is good—not even one." Another word for good is righteous. The word righteous means "one who is as he or she ought to be." Apart from Jesus Christ, we can not become the person we "ought to be."

2. Recognize that Jesus Christ died on the cross for you.

Scripture says, "But God showed His great love for us by sending Christ to die for us while we were still sinners." God gave His very son to die in our place when we least deserved it. As the Apostle Paul said, "(Christ) loved me and gave Himself for me …."

3. Repent of your sin

The Bible tells us to "repent and be converted." The word "repent" means to change our direction in life. Instead of running from God, we can run toward Him.

4. Receive Jesus Christ into your life.

Becoming a Christian is not merely believing some

creed or going to church on Sunday. It is having Christ Himself take residence in your life and heart. Jesus said, "Behold, I stand at the door (of your life) and knock. If anyone hears My voice and opens the door, I will come in ...."

Would you like Jesus Christ to come into your life right now? You might pray this suggested prayer:

"God, I am sorry for my sin. But I thank you for sending your Son, Jesus Christ, to die for me and to pay the price for my sin. I turn from it now and turn to you by faith. Come into my life and forgive me. I want to follow you from this time forward as your disciple. Thank you, Lord. In Jesus' name I pray."

Something you did not see in the movie ...

There is, finally, another little-known story about that fateful night. After the tragedy, some survivors spoke of an old preacher who had been a passenger on the Titanic. As the ship sank, he was thrown into the freezing Atlantic. When he realized he could not save his own life, he swam from lifeboat to lifeboat, raft to raft, piece of ship to piece of ship, crying out to the people, 'Trust Christ. Take Him as Savior. Receive Him into your heart. Call upon the name of the Lord and you will be saved.'"[15]

If you are looking for the meaning of starting, turning around, or operating a Christian school, this is it: Just Jesus! A Classic Excellence begins and ends with a singular, relentless, and passionate focus on Jesus Christ. Get this one thing right in your Christian school and watch God do wonderful things in your midst.

NOTES

[1] Larry Taylor, Things I Learned from My Pastor (Publisher: Costa Mesa, CA), p. 18.

[2] Arlin Horton, Pensacola Christian College, summer seminar Lecture, Pensacola, Florida, 1998.

[3] Leighton Ford, Transforming Leadership, (InterVarsity Press, Downers Grove, Illinois, 1991), p. 33.

[4] John Maxwell, Developing Leaders Around You, (Thomas Nelson Publishers, Nashville, Tennessee, 1995).

[5] Henry and Tom Blackaby, The Man God Uses, (Lifeway Press, Nashville, Tennessee, 1998), p. 137-140.

[6] Arlin Horton, Pensacola Christian College, *Summer Seminar Lecture*, Pensacola, Florida, 1998.

[7] L.B. Cowman, edited by; James Reimann, *Streams in the Desert, Zondervan Publishing House*, (Grand rapids, Michigan, 1997) p. 129-130.

[8] Loreen Itterman, *An Educator's Perspective*, National Institute for learning Disabilities, Brochure, Norfolk, VA.

[9] Mark Galli, Karl Barth, *Christian History, vol. XIX, no. 1 p. 25.*

[10] Basil Miller, George Mueller, *Man of Faith and Miracles*, Bethany House Publishers, Minneapolis, MN. p. 58-59.

[11] Russel Moldovan, Martin Luther King, Jr., *Christian History, vol. XIX, no.1. p. 40.*

[12] Henry Blackaby and Claude V. King, *Experiencing God*, Lifeway Press, Nashville, Tennessee, 1990.

[13] Janet Lowrie Nason, Selected Indicators of a Healthy Spiritual Culture in the Christian School (Christian School Education, vol. 3, issue 3, 1999-2000), p. 17-20.

[14] Greg Laurie, *Lessons from the Titanic*, Brochure